James Allen Collection - As a Man Thinketh, Eight Pillars of Prosperity, The Way of Peace and The Heavenly Life

James Allen Collection - As a Man Thinketh, Eight Pillars of Prosperity, The Way of Peace and The Heavenly Life

By

James Allen

Enhanced Media
2017

As a Man Thinketh by James Allen. First published in 1903. *Eight Pillars of Prosperity* by James Allen. First published in 1911. *The Way of Peace* by James Allen. First published in 1901. *The Heavenly Life* by James Allen. First published in 1903. *James Allen Collection - As a Man Thinketh, Eight Pillars of Prosperity, The Way of Peace and The Heavenly Life* published 2017 by Enhanced Media. All rights reserved.

Enhanced Media Publishing
Los Angeles, CA.

First Printing: 2017.

ISBN 978-1-365-78276-3

Contents

As a Man Thinketh 7
Thought and Character 8
Effect of Thought on Circumstances 10
Effect of Thought on Health and the Body 17
Thought and Purpose 19
The Thought-Factor in Achievement 21
Visions and Ideals 24
Serenity 27
Eight Pillars of Prosperity 29
The Way of Peace 97
The Heavenly Life 136

As a Man Thinketh

Mind is the Master power that moulds and makes,
And Man is Mind, and evermore he takes
The tool of Thought, and, shaping what he wills,
Brings forth a thousand joys, a thousand ills:—
He thinks in secret, and it comes to pass:
Environment is but his looking-glass.

THIS little volume (the result of meditation and experience) is not intended as an exhaustive treatise on the much-written-upon subject of the power of thought. It is suggestive rather than explanatory, its object being to stimulate men and women to the discovery and perception of the truth that—
"They themselves are makers of themselves."
by virtue of the thoughts, which they choose and encourage; that mind is the master-weaver, both of the inner garment of character and the outer garment of circumstance, and that, as they may have hitherto woven in ignorance and pain they may now weave in enlightenment and happiness.

JAMES ALLEN.
BROAD PARK AVENUE,
ILFRACOMBE,
ENGLAND

Thought and Character

THE aphorism, "As a man thinketh in his heart so is he," not only embraces the whole of a man's being, but is so comprehensive as to reach out to every condition and circumstance of his life. A man is literally what he thinks, his character being the complete sum of all his thoughts.

As the plant springs from, and could not be without, the seed, so every act of a man springs from the hidden seeds of thought, and could not have appeared without them. This applies equally to those acts called "spontaneous" and "unpremeditated" as to those, which are deliberately executed.

Act is the blossom of thought, and joy and suffering are its fruits; thus does a man garner in the sweet and bitter fruitage of his own husbandry.

"Thought in the mind hath made us, What we are
By thought was wrought and built. If a man's mind
Hath evil thoughts, pain comes on him as comes
The wheel the ox behind....

..If one endure
In purity of thought, joy follows him
As his own shadow—sure."

Man is a growth by law, and not a creation by artifice, and cause and effect is as absolute and undeviating in the hidden realm of thought as in the world of visible and material things. A noble and Godlike character is not a thing of favour or chance, but is the natural result of continued effort in right thinking, the effect of long-cherished association with Godlike thoughts. An ignoble and bestial character, by the same process, is the result of the continued harbouring of grovelling thoughts.

Man is made or unmade by himself; in the armoury of thought he forges the weapons by which he destroys himself; he also fashions the tools with which he builds for himself heavenly mansions of joy and strength and peace. By the right choice and true application of thought, man ascends to the Divine Perfection; by the abuse and wrong application of thought, he descends below the level of the beast. Between these two extremes are all the grades of character, and man is their maker and master.

Of all the beautiful truths pertaining to the soul which have been restored and brought to light in this age, none is more gladdening or fruitful of divine promise and confidence than this—that man is the master of thought, the moulder of character, and the maker and shaper of condition, environment, and destiny.

As a being of Power, Intelligence, and Love, and the lord of his own thoughts, man holds the key to every situation, and contains within himself that transforming and regenerative agency by which he may make himself what he wills.

Man is always the master, even in his weaker and most abandoned state; but in his weakness and degradation he is the foolish master who misgoverns his "household." When he begins to reflect upon his condition, and to search diligently for the Law upon which his being is established, he then becomes the wise master, directing his energies with intelligence, and fashioning his thoughts to fruitful issues. Such is the conscious master, and man can only thus become by discovering within himself the laws of thought; which discovery is totally a matter of application, self-analysis, and experience.

Only by much searching and mining, are gold and diamonds obtained, and man can find every truth connected with his being, if he will dig deep into the mine of his soul; and that he is the maker of his character, the moulder of his life, and the builder of his destiny, he may unerringly prove, if he will watch, control, and alter his thoughts, tracing their effects upon himself, upon others, and upon his life and circumstances, linking cause and effect by patient practice and investigation, and utilizing his every experience, even to the most trivial, everyday occurrence, as a means of obtaining that knowledge of himself which is Understanding, Wisdom, Power. In this direction, as in no other, is the law absolute that "He that seeketh findeth; and to him that knocketh it shall be opened;" for only by patience, practice, and ceaseless importunity can a man enter the Door of the Temple of Knowledge.

Effect of Thought on Circumstances

MAN'S mind may be likened to a garden, which may be intelligently cultivated or allowed to run wild; but whether cultivated or neglected, it must, and will, bring forth. If no useful seeds are put into it, then an abundance of useless weed-seeds will fall therein, and will continue to produce their kind.

Just as a gardener cultivates his plot, keeping it free from weeds, and growing the flowers and fruits which he requires, so may a man tend the garden of his mind, weeding out all the wrong, useless, and impure thoughts, and cultivating toward perfection the flowers and fruits of right, useful, and pure thoughts. By pursuing this process, a man sooner or later discovers that he is the master-gardener of his soul, the director of his life. He also reveals, within himself, the laws of thought, and understands, with ever-increasing accuracy, how the thought-forces and mind elements operate in the shaping of his character, circumstances, and destiny.

Thought and character are one, and as character can only manifest and discover itself through environment and circumstance, the outer conditions of a person's life will always be found to be harmoniously related to his inner state. This does not mean that a man's circumstances at any given time are an indication of his entire character, but that those circumstances are so intimately connected with some vital thought-element within himself that, for the time being, they are indispensable to his development.

Every man is where he is by the law of his being; the thoughts which he has built into his character have brought him there, and in the arrangement of his life there is no element of chance, but all is the result of a law which cannot err. This is just as true of those who feel "out of harmony" with their surroundings as of those who are contented with them.

As a progressive and evolving being, man is where he is that he may learn that he may grow; and as he learns the spiritual lesson which any circumstance contains for him, it passes away and gives place to other circumstances.

Man is buffeted by circumstances so long as he believes himself to be the creature of outside conditions, but when he realizes that he is a creative power, and that he may command the hidden soil and seeds of his being out of which circumstances grow, he then becomes the rightful master of himself.

That circumstances grow out of thought every man knows who has for any length of time practised self-control and self-purification, for he will have noticed that the alteration in his circumstances has been in exact ratio with his altered mental condition. So true is this that when a man earnestly applies himself to remedy the defects in his character, and makes swift and marked progress, he passes rapidly through a succession of vicissitudes.

The soul attracts that which it secretly harbours; that which it loves, and also that which it fears; it reaches the height of its cherished aspirations; it falls to the level of its unchastened desires,—and circumstances are the means by which the soul receives its own.

Every thought-seed sown or allowed to fall into the mind, and to take root there, produces its own, blossoming sooner or later into act, and bearing its own fruitage of opportunity and circumstance. Good thoughts bear good fruit, bad thoughts bad fruit.

The outer world of circumstance shapes itself to the inner world of thought, and both pleasant and unpleasant external conditions are factors, which make for the ultimate good of the individual. As the reaper of his own harvest, man learns both by suffering and bliss.

Following the inmost desires, aspirations, thoughts, by which he allows himself to be dominated, (pursuing the will-o'-the-wisps of impure imaginings or steadfastly walking the highway of strong and high endeavour), a man at last arrives at their fruition and fulfilment in the outer conditions of his life. The laws of growth and adjustment everywhere obtains.

A man does not come to the almshouse or the jail by the tyranny of fate or circumstance, but by the pathway of grovelling thoughts and base desires. Nor does a pure-minded man fall suddenly into crime by stress of any mere external force; the criminal thought had long been secretly fostered in the heart, and the hour of opportunity revealed its gathered power. Circumstance does not make the man; it reveals him to himself No such conditions can exist as descending into vice and its attendant sufferings apart from vicious inclinations, or ascending into virtue and its pure happiness without the continued cultivation of virtuous aspirations; and man, therefore, as the lord and master of thought, is the maker of himself the shaper and author of environment. Even at birth the soul comes to its own and through every step of its earthly pilgrimage it attracts those combinations of conditions which reveal itself, which are the reflections of its own purity and, impurity, its strength and weakness.

Men do not attract that which they want, but that which they are. Their whims, fancies, and ambitions are thwarted at every step, but their inmost thoughts and desires are fed with their own food, be it foul or clean. The "divinity that shapes our ends" is in ourselves; it is our very self. Only himself manacles man: thought and action are the gaolers of Fate—they imprison, being base; they are also the angels of Freedom—they liberate, being noble. Not what he wishes and prays for does a man get, but what he justly earns. His wishes and prayers are only gratified and answered when they harmonize with his thoughts and actions.

In the light of this truth, what, then, is the meaning of "fighting against circumstances?" It means that a man is continually revolting against an effect without, while all the time he is nourishing and preserving its cause in his heart. That cause may take the form of a conscious vice or an unconscious weakness; but whatever it is, it stubbornly retards the efforts of its possessor, and thus calls aloud for remedy.

Men are anxious to improve their circumstances, but are unwilling to improve themselves; they therefore remain bound. The man who does not shrink from self-crucifixion can never fail to accomplish the object upon which his heart is set. This is as true of earthly as of heavenly things. Even the man whose sole object is to acquire wealth must be prepared to make great personal sacrifices before he can accomplish his object; and how much more so he who would realize a strong and well-poised life?

Here is a man who is wretchedly poor. He is extremely anxious that his surroundings and home comforts should be improved, yet all the time he shirks his work, and considers he is justified in trying to deceive his employer on the ground of the insufficiency of his wages. Such a man does not understand the simplest rudiments of those principles which are the basis of true prosperity, and is not only totally unfitted to rise out of his wretchedness, but is actually attracting to himself a still deeper wretchedness by dwelling in, and acting out, indolent, deceptive, and unmanly thoughts.

Here is a rich man who is the victim of a painful and persistent disease as the result of gluttony. He is willing to give large sums of money to get rid of it, but he will not sacrifice his gluttonous desires. He wants to gratify his taste for rich and unnatural viands and have his health as well. Such a man is totally unfit to have health, because he has not yet learned the first principles of a healthy life.

Here is an employer of labour who adopts crooked measures to avoid paying the regulation wage, and, in the hope of making larger profits, reduces the wages of his workpeople. Such a man is altogether unfitted for prosperity, and when he finds himself bankrupt, both as regards reputation and riches, he blames circumstances, not knowing that he is the sole author of his condition.

I have introduced these three cases merely as illustrative of the truth that man is the causer (though nearly always is unconsciously) of his circumstances, and that, whilst aiming at a good end, he is continually frustrating its accomplishment by encouraging thoughts and desires which cannot possibly harmonize with that end. Such cases could be multiplied and varied almost indefinitely, but this is not necessary, as the reader can, if he so resolves, trace the action of the laws of thought in his own mind and life, and until this is done, mere external facts cannot serve as a ground of reasoning.

Circumstances, however, are so complicated, thought is so deeply rooted, and the conditions of happiness vary so, vastly with individuals, that a man's entire soul-condition (although it may be known to himself) cannot be judged by another from the external aspect of his life alone. A man may be honest in certain directions, yet suffer privations; a man may be dishonest in certain directions, yet acquire wealth; but the conclusion usually formed that the one man fails because of his particular honesty, and that the other prospers because of his particular dishonesty, is the result of a superficial judgment, which assumes that the dishonest man is almost totally corrupt, and the honest man almost entirely virtuous. In the light of a deeper knowledge and wider experience such judgment is found to be erroneous. The dishonest man may have some admirable virtues, which the other does, not possess; and the honest man obnoxious vices which are absent in the other. The honest man reaps the good results of his honest thoughts and acts; he also brings upon himself the sufferings, which his vices produce. The dishonest man likewise garners his own suffering and happiness.

It is pleasing to human vanity to believe that one suffers because of one's virtue; but not until a man has extirpated every sickly, bitter, and impure thought from his mind, and washed every sinful stain from his soul, can he be in a position to know and declare that his sufferings are the result of his good, and not of his bad qualities; and on the way to, yet long before he has reached, that supreme perfection, he will have found, working in his mind and life, the Great Law which is absolutely just, and which cannot, therefore, give good for evil, evil for good. Possessed of such knowledge, he will then know, looking back upon his past ignorance and blindness, that his life is, and always was, justly ordered, and that all his past experiences, good and bad, were the equitable outworking of his evolving, yet unevolved self.

Good thoughts and actions can never produce bad results; bad thoughts and actions can never produce good results. This is but saying that nothing can come from corn but corn, nothing from nettles but nettles. Men understand this law in the natural world, and work with it; but few understand it in the mental and moral world (though its operation there is just as simple and undeviating), and they, therefore, do not co-operate with it.

Suffering is always the effect of wrong thought in some direction. It is an indication that the individual is out of harmony with himself, with the

Law of his being. The sole and supreme use of suffering is to purify, to burn out all that is useless and impure. Suffering ceases for him who is pure. There could be no object in burning gold after the dross had been removed, and a perfectly pure and enlightened being could not suffer.

The circumstances, which a man encounters with suffering, are the result of his own mental in harmony. The circumstances, which a man encounters with blessedness, are the result of his own mental harmony. Blessedness, not material possessions, is the measure of right thought; wretchedness, not lack of material possessions, is the measure of wrong thought. A man may be cursed and rich; he may be blessed and poor. Blessedness and riches are only joined together when the riches are rightly and wisely used; and the poor man only descends into wretchedness when he regards his lot as a burden unjustly imposed.

Indigence and indulgence are the two extremes of wretchedness. They are both equally unnatural and the result of mental disorder. A man is not rightly conditioned until he is a happy, healthy, and prosperous being; and happiness, health, and prosperity are the result of a harmonious adjustment of the inner with the outer, of the man with his surroundings.

A man only begins to be a man when he ceases to whine and revile, and commences to search for the hidden justice which regulates his life. And as he adapts his mind to that regulating factor, he ceases to accuse others as the cause of his condition, and builds himself up in strong and noble thoughts; ceases to kick against circumstances, but begins to use them as aids to his more rapid progress, and as a means of discovering the hidden powers and possibilities within himself.

Law, not confusion, is the dominating principle in the universe; justice, not injustice, is the soul and substance of life; and righteousness, not corruption, is the moulding and moving force in the spiritual government of the world. This being so, man has but to right himself to find that the universe is right; and during the process of putting himself right he will find that as he alters his thoughts towards things and other people, things and other people will alter towards him.

The proof of this truth is in every person, and it therefore admits of easy investigation by systematic introspection and self-analysis. Let a man radically alter his thoughts, and he will be astonished at the rapid transformation it will effect in the material conditions of his life. Men imagine that thought can be kept secret, but it cannot; it rapidly crystallizes into habit, and habit solidifies into circumstance. Bestial thoughts crystallize into habits of drunkenness and sensuality, which solidify into circumstances of destitution and disease: impure thoughts of every kind crystallize into enervating and confusing habits, which solidify into distracting and adverse circumstances: thoughts of fear, doubt, and indecision crystallize into weak, unmanly, and irresolute habits, which solidify into circumstances of failure, indigence, and slavish dependence: lazy thoughts crystallize into habits of uncleanliness and dishonesty, which solidify into circumstances of foulness and beggary: hateful and condemnatory thoughts crystallize into habits of accusation and violence, which solidify into circumstances of injury and persecution: selfish thoughts of all kinds crystallize into habits of self-seeking, which solidify into circumstances more or less distressing. On the other hand, beautiful thoughts of all kinds crystallize into habits of grace and kindliness, which solidify into genial and sunny circumstances: pure thoughts crystallize into habits of temperance and self-control, which solidify into circumstances of repose and peace: thoughts of courage, self-reliance, and decision crystallize into manly habits, which solidify into circumstances of success, plenty, and freedom: energetic thoughts crystallize into habits of cleanliness and industry, which solidify into circumstances of pleasantness: gentle and forgiving thoughts crystallize into habits of gentleness, which solidify into protective and preservative circumstances: loving and unselfish thoughts crystallize into habits of self-forgetfulness for others, which solidify into circumstances of sure and abiding prosperity and true riches.

A particular train of thought persisted in, be it good or bad, cannot fail to produce its results on the character and circumstances. A man cannot directly choose his circumstances, but he can choose his thoughts, and so indirectly, yet surely, shape his circumstances.

Nature helps every man to the gratification of the thoughts, which he most encourages, and opportunities are presented which will most speedily bring to the surface both the good and evil thoughts.

Let a man cease from his sinful thoughts, and all the world will soften towards him, and be ready to help him; let him put away his weakly and sickly thoughts, and lo, opportunities will spring up on every hand to aid his strong resolves; let him encourage good thoughts, and no hard fate shall bind him down to wretchedness and shame. The world is your kaleidoscope, and the varying combinations of colours, which at every succeeding moment it presents to you are the exquisitely adjusted pictures of your ever-moving thoughts.

"So You will be what you will to be;
Let failure find its false content
In that poor word, 'environment,'
But spirit scorns it, and is free.

"It masters time, it conquers space;
It cowes that boastful trickster, Chance,
And bids the tyrant Circumstance
Uncrown, and fill a servant's place.

"The human Will, that force unseen,
The offspring of a deathless Soul,
Can hew a way to any goal,
Though walls of granite intervene.

"Be not impatient in delays
But wait as one who understands;
When spirit rises and commands
The gods are ready to obey."

Effect of Thought on Health and the Body

THE body is the servant of the mind. It obeys the operations of the mind, whether they be deliberately chosen or automatically expressed. At the bidding of unlawful thoughts the body sinks rapidly into disease and decay; at the command of glad and beautiful thoughts it becomes clothed with youthfulness and beauty.

Disease and health, like circumstances, are rooted in thought. Sickly thoughts will express themselves through a sickly body. Thoughts of fear have been known to kill a man as speedily as a bullet, and they are continually killing thousands of people just as surely though less rapidly. The people who live in fear of disease are the people who get it. Anxiety quickly demoralizes the whole body, and lays it open to the entrance of disease; while impure thoughts, even if not physically indulged, will soon shatter the nervous system.

Strong, pure, and happy thoughts build up the body in vigour and grace. The body is a delicate and plastic instrument, which responds readily to the thoughts by which it is impressed, and habits of thought will produce their own effects, good or bad, upon it.

Men will continue to have impure and poisoned blood, so long as they propagate unclean thoughts. Out of a clean heart comes a clean life and a clean body. Out of a defiled mind proceeds a defiled life and a corrupt body. Thought is the fount of action, life, and manifestation; make the fountain pure, and all will be pure.

Change of diet will not help a man who will not change his thoughts. When a man makes his thoughts pure, he no longer desires impure food.

Clean thoughts make clean habits. The so-called saint who does not wash his body is not a saint. He who has strengthened and purified his thoughts does not need to consider the malevolent microbe.

If you would protect your body, guard your mind. If you would renew your body, beautify your mind. Thoughts of malice, envy, disappointment, despondency, rob the body of its health and grace. A sour face does not come by chance; it is made by sour thoughts. Wrinkles that mar are drawn by folly, passion, and pride.

I know a woman of ninety-six who has the bright, innocent face of a girl. I know a man well under middle age whose face is drawn into inharmonious contours. The one is the result of a sweet and sunny disposition; the other is the outcome of passion and discontent.

As you cannot have a sweet and wholesome abode unless you admit the air and sunshine freely into your rooms, so a strong body and a bright, happy, or serene countenance can only result from the free admittance into the mind of thoughts of joy and goodwill and serenity.

On the faces of the aged there are wrinkles made by sympathy, others by strong and pure thought, and others are carved by passion: who cannot distinguish them? With those who have lived righteously, age is calm, peaceful, and softly mellowed, like the setting sun. I have recently seen a philosopher on his deathbed. He was not old except in years. He died as sweetly and peacefully as he had lived.

There is no physician like cheerful thought for dissipating the ills of the body; there is no comforter to compare with goodwill for dispersing the shadows of grief and sorrow. To live continually in thoughts of ill will, cynicism, suspicion, and envy, is to be confined in a self-made prison-hole. But to think well of all, to be cheerful with all, to patiently learn to find the good in all—such unselfish thoughts are the very portals of heaven; and to dwell day by day in thoughts of peace toward every creature will bring abounding peace to their possessor.

Thought and Purpose

UNTIL thought is linked with purpose there is no intelligent accomplishment. With the majority the bark of thought is allowed to "drift" upon the ocean of life. Aimlessness is a vice, and such drifting must not continue for him who would steer clear of catastrophe and destruction.

They who have no central purpose in their life fall an easy prey to petty worries, fears, troubles, and self-pityings, all of which are indications of weakness, which lead, just as surely as deliberately planned sins (though by a different route), to failure, unhappiness, and loss, for weakness cannot persist in a power evolving universe.

A man should conceive of a legitimate purpose in his heart, and set out to accomplish it. He should make this purpose the centralizing point of his thoughts. It may take the form of a spiritual ideal, or it may be a worldly object, according to his nature at the time being; but whichever it is, he should steadily focus his thought-forces upon the object, which he has set before him. He should make this purpose his supreme duty, and should devote himself to its attainment, not allowing his thoughts to wander away into ephemeral fancies, longings, and imaginings. This is the royal road to self-control and true concentration of thought. Even if he fails again and again to accomplish his purpose (as he necessarily must until weakness is overcome), the strength of character gained will be the measure of his true success, and this will form a new starting-point for future power and triumph.

Those who are not prepared for the apprehension of a great purpose should fix the thoughts upon the faultless performance of their duty, no matter how insignificant their task may appear. Only in this way can the thoughts be gathered and focussed, and resolution and energy be developed, which being done, there is nothing which may not be accomplished.

The weakest soul, knowing its own weakness, and believing this truth that strength can only be developed by effort and practice, will, thus believing, at once begin to exert itself, and, adding effort to effort, patience to patience, and strength to strength, will never cease to develop, and will at last grow divinely strong.

As the physically weak man can make himself strong by careful and patient training, so the man of weak thoughts can make them strong by exercising himself in right thinking.

To put away aimlessness and weakness, and to begin to think with purpose, is to enter the ranks of those strong ones who only recognize failure as one of the pathways to attainment; who make all conditions serve them, and who think strongly, attempt fearlessly, and accomplish masterfully.

Having conceived of his purpose, a man should mentally mark out a straight pathway to its achievement, looking neither to the right nor the left. Doubts and fears should be rigorously excluded; they are disintegrating elements, which break up the straight line of effort, rendering it crooked, ineffectual, useless. Thoughts of doubt and fear never accomplished anything, and never can. They always lead to failure. Purpose, energy, power to do, and all strong thoughts cease when doubt and fear creep in.

The will to do springs from the knowledge that we can do. Doubt and fear are the great enemies of knowledge, and he who encourages them, who does not slay them, thwarts himself at every step.

He who has conquered doubt and fear has conquered failure. His every thought is allied with power, and all difficulties are bravely met and wisely overcome. His purposes are seasonably planted, and they bloom and bring forth fruit, which does not fall prematurely to the ground.

Thought allied fearlessly to purpose becomes creative force: he who knows this is ready to become something higher and stronger than a mere bundle of wavering thoughts and fluctuating sensations; he who does this has become the conscious and intelligent wielder of his mental powers.

The Thought-Factor in Achievement

ALL that a man achieves and all that he fails to achieve is the direct result of his own thoughts. In a justly ordered universe, where loss of equipoise would mean total destruction, individual responsibility must be absolute. A man's weakness and strength, purity and impurity, are his own, and not another man's; they are brought about by himself, and not by another; and they can only be altered by himself, never by another. His condition is also his own, and not another man's. His suffering and his happiness are evolved from within. As he thinks, so he is; as he continues to think, so he remains.

A strong man cannot help a weaker unless that weaker is willing to be helped, and even then the weak man must become strong of himself; he must, by his own efforts, develop the strength which he admires in another. None but himself can alter his condition.

It has been usual for men to think and to say, "Many men are slaves because one is an oppressor; let us hate the oppressor." Now, however, there is amongst an increasing few a tendency to reverse this judgment, and to say, "One man is an oppressor because many are slaves; let us despise the slaves."

The truth is that oppressor and slave are co-operators in ignorance, and, while seeming to afflict each other, are in reality afflicting themselves. A perfect Knowledge perceives the action of law in the weakness of the oppressed and the misapplied power of the oppressor; a perfect Love, seeing the suffering, which both states entail, condemns neither; a perfect Compassion embraces both oppressor and oppressed.

He who has conquered weakness, and has put away all selfish thoughts, belongs neither to oppressor nor oppressed. He is free.

A man can only rise, conquer, and achieve by lifting up his thoughts. He can only remain weak, and abject, and miserable by refusing to lift up his thoughts.

Before a man can achieve anything, even in worldly things, he must lift his thoughts above slavish animal indulgence. He may not, in order to succeed, give up all animality and selfishness, by any means; but a portion of it must, at least, be sacrificed. A man whose first thought is bestial indulgence could neither think clearly nor plan methodically; he could not find and develop his latent resources, and would fail in any undertaking. Not having commenced to manfully control his thoughts, he is not in a position to control affairs and to adopt serious responsibilities. He is not fit to act independently and stand alone. But he is limited only by the thoughts, which he chooses.

There can be no progress, no achievement without sacrifice, and a man's worldly success will be in the measure that he sacrifices his confused animal thoughts, and fixes his mind on the development of his plans, and the strengthening of his resolution and self-reliance. And the higher he lifts his thoughts, the more manly, upright, and righteous he becomes, the greater will be his success, the more blessed and enduring will be his achievements.

The universe does not favour the greedy, the dishonest, the vicious, although on the mere surface it may sometimes appear to do so; it helps the honest, the magnanimous, the virtuous. All the great Teachers of the ages have declared this in varying forms, and to prove and know it a man has but to persist in making himself more and more virtuous by lifting up his thoughts.

Intellectual achievements are the result of thought consecrated to the search for knowledge, or for the beautiful and true in life and nature. Such achievements may be sometimes connected with vanity and ambition, but they are not the outcome of those characteristics; they are the natural outgrowth of long and arduous effort, and of pure and unselfish thoughts.

Spiritual achievements are the consummation of holy aspirations. He who lives constantly in the conception of noble and lofty thoughts, who dwells upon all that is pure and unselfish, will, as surely as the sun reaches its zenith and the moon its full, become wise and noble in character, and rise into a position of influence and blessedness.

Achievement, of whatever kind, is the crown of effort, the diadem of thought. By the aid of self-control, resolution, purity, righteousness, and well-directed thought a man ascends; by the aid of animality, indolence, impurity, corruption, and confusion of thought a man descends.

A man may rise to high success in the world, and even to lofty altitudes in the spiritual realm, and again descend into weakness and wretchedness by allowing arrogant, selfish, and corrupt thoughts to take possession of him.

Victories attained by right thought can only be maintained by watchfulness. Many give way when success is assured, and rapidly fall back into failure.

All achievements, whether in the business, intellectual, or spiritual world, are the result of definitely directed thought, are governed by the same law and are of the same method; the only difference lies in the object of attainment.

He who would accomplish little must sacrifice little; he who would achieve much must sacrifice much; he who would attain highly must sacrifice greatly.

Visions and Ideals

THE dreamers are the saviours of the world. As the visible world is sustained by the invisible, so men, through all their trials and sins and sordid vocations, are nourished by the beautiful visions of their solitary dreamers. Humanity cannot forget its dreamers; it cannot let their ideals fade and die; it lives in them; it knows them as the realities which it shall one day see and know.

Composer, sculptor, painter, poet, prophet, sage, these are the makers of the after-world, the architects of heaven. The world is beautiful because they have lived; without them, labouring humanity would perish.

He who cherishes a beautiful vision, a lofty ideal in his heart, will one day realize it. Columbus cherished a vision of another world, and he discovered it; Copernicus fostered the vision of a multiplicity of worlds and a wider universe, and he revealed it; Buddha beheld the vision of a spiritual world of stainless beauty and perfect peace, and he entered into it.

Cherish your visions; cherish your ideals; cherish the music that stirs in your heart, the beauty that forms in your mind, the loveliness that drapes your purest thoughts, for out of them will grow all delightful conditions, all, heavenly environment; of these, if you but remain true to them, your world will at last be built.

To desire is to obtain; to aspire is to, achieve. Shall man's basest desires receive the fullest measure of gratification, and his purest aspirations starve for lack of sustenance? Such is not the Law: such a condition of things can never obtain: "ask and receive."

Dream lofty dreams, and as you dream, so shall you become. Your Vision is the promise of what you shall one day be; your Ideal is the prophecy of what you shall at last unveil.

The greatest achievement was at first and for a time a dream. The oak sleeps in the acorn; the bird waits in the egg; and in the highest vision of the soul a waking angel stirs. Dreams are the seedlings of realities.

Your circumstances may be uncongenial, but they shall not long remain so if you but perceive an Ideal and strive to reach it. You cannot travel within and stand still without. Here is a youth hard pressed by poverty and labour; confined long hours in an unhealthy workshop; unschooled, and lacking all the arts of refinement. But he dreams of better things; he thinks of intelligence, of refinement, of grace and beauty. He conceives of, mentally builds up, an ideal condition of life; the vision of a wider liberty and a larger scope takes possession of him; unrest urges him to action, and he utilizes all his spare time and means, small though they are, to the development of his latent powers and resources. Very soon so altered has his mind become that the workshop can no longer hold him. It has become so out of harmony with his mentality that it falls out of his life as a garment is cast aside, and, with the growth of opportunities, which fit the scope of his expanding powers, he passes out of it forever. Years later we see this youth as a full-grown man. We find him a master of certain forces of the mind, which he wields with worldwide influence and almost unequalled power. In his hands he holds the cords of gigantic responsibilities; he speaks, and lo, lives are changed; men and women hang upon his words and remould their characters, and, sunlike, he becomes the fixed and luminous centre round which innumerable destinies revolve. He has realized the Vision of his youth. He has become one with his Ideal.

And you, too, youthful reader, will realize the Vision (not the idle wish) of your heart, be it base or beautiful, or a mixture of both, for you will always gravitate toward that which you, secretly, most love. Into your hands will be placed the exact results of your own thoughts; you will receive that which you earn; no more, no less. Whatever your present environment may be, you will fall, remain, or rise with your thoughts, your Vision, your Ideal. You will become as small as your controlling desire; as great as your dominant aspiration: in the beautiful words of Stanton Kirkham Davis, "You may be keeping accounts, and presently you shall walk out of the door that for so long has seemed to you the barrier of your ideals, and shall find yourself before an audience—the pen still behind your ear, the ink stains on your fingers and then and there shall pour out the torrent of your inspiration. You may be driving sheep, and you shall wander to the city-bucolic and open-mouthed; shall wander under the intrepid guidance of the spirit into the studio of the master, and after a time he shall say, 'I have nothing more to teach you.' And now you have become the master, who did so recently dream of great things while driving sheep. You shall lay down the saw and the plane to take upon yourself the regeneration of the world."

The thoughtless, the ignorant, and the indolent, seeing only the apparent effects of things and not the things themselves, talk of luck, of fortune, and chance. Seeing a man grow rich, they say, "How lucky he is!" Observing another become intellectual, they exclaim, "How highly favoured he is!" And noting the saintly character and wide influence of another, they remark, "How chance aids him at every turn!" They do not see the trials and failures and struggles which these men have voluntarily encountered in order to gain their experience; have no knowledge of the sacrifices they have made, of the undaunted efforts they have put forth, of the faith they have exercised, that they might overcome the apparently insurmountable, and realize the Vision of their heart. They do not know the darkness and the heartaches; they only see the light and joy, and call it "luck". They do not see the long and arduous journey, but only behold the pleasant goal, and call it "good fortune," do not understand the process, but only perceive the result, and call it chance.

In all human affairs there are efforts, and there are results, and the strength of the effort is the measure of the result. Chance is not. Gifts, powers, material, intellectual, and spiritual possessions are the fruits of effort; they are thoughts completed, objects accomplished, visions realized.

The Vision that you glorify in your mind, the Ideal that you enthrone in your heart—this you will build your life by, this you will become.

Serenity

CALMNESS of mind is one of the beautiful jewels of wisdom. It is the result of long and patient effort in self-control. Its presence is an indication of ripened experience, and of a more than ordinary knowledge of the laws and operations of thought.

A man becomes calm in the measure that he understands himself as a thought evolved being, for such knowledge necessitates the understanding of others as the result of thought, and as he develops a right understanding, and sees more and more clearly the internal relations of things by the action of cause and effect he ceases to fuss and fume and worry and grieve, and remains poised, steadfast, serene.

The calm man, having learned how to govern himself, knows how to adapt himself to others; and they, in turn, reverence his spiritual strength, and feel that they can learn of him and rely upon him. The more tranquil a man becomes, the greater is his success, his influence, his power for good. Even the ordinary trader will find his business prosperity increase as he develops a greater self-control and equanimity, for people will always prefer to deal with a man whose demeanour is strongly equable.

The strong, calm man is always loved and revered. He is like a shade-giving tree in a thirsty land, or a sheltering rock in a storm. "Who does not love a tranquil heart, a sweet-tempered, balanced life? It does not matter whether it rains or shines, or what changes come to those possessing these blessings, for they are always sweet, serene, and calm. That exquisite poise of character, which we call serenity is the last lesson of culture, the fruitage of the soul. It is precious as wisdom, more to be desired than gold—yea, than even fine gold. How insignificant mere money seeking looks in comparison with a serene life—a life that dwells in the ocean of Truth, beneath the waves, beyond the reach of tempests, in the Eternal Calm!

"How many people we know who sour their lives, who ruin all that is sweet and beautiful by explosive tempers, who destroy their poise of character, and make bad blood! It is a question whether the great majority of people do not ruin their lives and mar their happiness by lack of self-control. How few people we meet in life who are well balanced, who have that exquisite poise which is characteristic of the finished character!

Yes, humanity surges with uncontrolled passion, is tumultuous with ungoverned grief, is blown about by anxiety and doubt only the wise man, only he whose thoughts are controlled and purified, makes the winds and the storms of the soul obey him.

Tempest-tossed souls, wherever ye may be, under whatsoever conditions ye may live, know this in the ocean of life the isles of Blessedness are smiling, and the sunny shore of your ideal awaits your coming. Keep your hand firmly upon the helm of thought. In the bark of your soul reclines the commanding Master; He does but sleep: wake Him. Self-control is strength; Right Thought is mastery; Calmness is power. Say unto your heart, "Peace, be still!"

Eight Pillars of Prosperity

Preface

It is popularly supposed that a greater prosperity for individuals or nations can only come through a political and social reconstruction. This cannot be true apart from the practice of the moral virtues in the individuals that comprise a nation. Better laws and social conditions will always follow a higher realisation of morality among the individuals of a community, but no legal enactment can give prosperity to, nay it cannot prevent the ruin of, a man or a nation that has become lax and decadent in the pursuit and practice of virtue.

The moral virtues are the foundation and support of prosperity as they are the soul of greatness. They endure for ever, and all the works of man which endure are built upon them. Without them there is neither strength, stability, nor substantial reality, but only ephemeral dreams. To find moral principles is to have found prosperity, greatness, truth, and is therefore to be strong, valiant, joyful and free.

JAMES ALLEN
"Bryngoleu,"
Ilfracombe,
England.

1. Eight pillars

Prosperity rests upon a moral foundation. It is popularly supposed to rest upon an immoral foundation - that is, upon trickery, sharp practice, deception and greed. One commonly hears even an otherwise intelligent man declare that "No man can be successful in business unless he is dishonest," thus regarding business prosperity – a good thing – as the effect of dishonesty – a bad thing. Such a statement is superficial and thoughtless, and reveals a total lack of knowledge of moral causation, as well as a very limited grasp of the facts of life. It is as though one should sow henbane and reap spinach, or erect a brick house on a quagmire - things impossible in the natural order of causation, and therefore not to be attempted. The spiritual or moral order of causation is not different in principle, but only in nature. The same law obtains in things unseen – in thoughts and deeds - as in things seen – in natural phenomena. Man sees the processes in natural objects, and acts in ac-accordance with them, but not seeing the spiritual processes, he imagines that they do not obtain, and so he does not act in harmony with them.

Yet these spiritual processes are just as simple and just as sure as the natural processes. They are indeed the same natural modes manifesting in the world of mind. All the parables and a large number of the sayings of the Great Teachers are designed to illustrate this fact. The natural world is the mental world made visible. The seen is the mirror of the unseen. The upper half of a circle is in no way different from the lower half, but its sphericity is reversed. The material and the mental are not two detached arcs in the universe, they are the two halves of a complete circle. The natural and the spiritual are not at eternal enmity, but in the true order of the universe are eternally at one. It is in the unnatural - in the abuse of function and faculty – where division arises, and where main is wrested back, with repeated sufferings, from the perfect circle from which he has tried to depart. Every process in matter is also a process in mind. Every natural law has its spiritual counterpart.

Take any natural object, and you will find its fundamental processes in the mental sphere if you rightly search. Consider, for instance, the germination of a seed and its growth into a plant with the final development of a flower, and back to seed again. This also is a mental process. Thoughts are seeds which, falling in the soil of the mind, germinate and develop until they reach the completed stage, blossoming into deeds good or bad, brilliant or stupid, according to their nature, and ending as seeds of thought to be again sown in other minds. A teacher is a sower of seed, a spiritual agriculturist, while he who teaches himself is the wise farmer of his own mental plot. The growth of a thought is as the growth of a plant. The seed must be sown seasonably, and time is required for its full development into the plant of knowledge and the flower of wisdom.

While writing this, I pause, and turn to look through my study window, and there, a hundred yards away, is a tall tree in the top of which some enterprising rook from a rookery hard by, has, for the first time, built its nest. A strong, north-east wind is blowing, so that the top of the tree is swayed violently to and fro by the onset of the blast; yet there is no danger to that frail thing of sticks and hair, and the mother bird, sitting upon her eggs, has no fear of the storm. Why is this? It is because the bird has instinctively built her nest in harmony with principles which ensure the maximum strength and security. First, a fork is chosen as the foundation for the nest, and not a space between two separate branches, so that, however great may be the swaying of the tree top, the position of the nest is not altered, nor its structure disturbed; then the nest is built on a circular plan so as to offer the greatest resistance to any external pressure, as well as to obtain more perfect compactness within, in accordance with its purpose; and so, however the tempest may rage, the birds rest in comfort and security. This is a very simple and familiar object, and yet, in the strict obedience of its structure to mathematical law, it becomes, to the wise, a parable of enlightenment, teaching them that only by ordering one's deeds in accordance with fixed principles is perfect surety, perfect security, and perfect peace obtained amid the uncertainty of events and the turbulent tempests of life.

A house or a temple built by man is a much more complicated structure than a bird's nest, yet it is erected in accordance with those mathematical principles which are everywhere evidenced in nature. And here is seen how man, in material things, obeys universal principles. He never attempts to put up a building in defiance of geometrical proportions, for he knows that such a building would be unsafe, and that the first storm would, in all probability, level it to the ground, if, indeed, it did not fall about his ears during the process of erection. Man in his material building scrupulously obeys the fixed principles of circle, square and angle, and, aided by rule, plumbline, and compasses, he raises a structure which will resist the fiercest storms, and afford him a secure shelter and safe protection.

All this is very simple, the reader may say. Yes, it is simple because it is true and perfect; so true that it cannot admit the smallest compromise, and so perfect that no man can improve upon it. Man, through long experience, has learned these principles of the material world, and sees the wisdom of obeying them, and I have thus referred to them in order to lead up to a consideration of those fixed principles in the mental or spiritual world which are just as simple, and just as eternally true and perfect, yet are at present so little understood by man that he daily violates them, because ignorant of their nature, and unconscious of the harm he is all the time inflicting upon himself.

In mind as in matter, in thoughts as in things, in deeds as in natural processes, there is a fixed foundation of law which, if consciously or ignorantly ignored leads to disaster, and defeat. It is, indeed, the ignorant violation of this law which is the cause of the world's pain and sorrow. In matter, this law is presented as mathematical; in mind, it is perceived as moral. But the mathematical and the moral are not separate and opposed; they are but two aspects of a united whole. The fixed principles of mathematics, to which all matter is subject, are the body of which the spirit is ethical; while the eternal principles of morality are mathematical truisms operating in the universe of mind. It is as impossible to live successfully apart from moral principles, as to build successfully while ignoring mathematical principles. Characters, like houses, only stand firmly when built on a foundation of moral law - and they are built up slowly and laboriously, deed by deed, for in the building of character, the bricks are deeds. Business and all human enterprises are not exempt from the eternal order, but can only stand securely by the observance of fixed laws. Prosperity, to be stable and enduring, must rest on a solid foundation of moral principle, and be supported by the adamantine pillars of sterling character and moral worth. In the attempt to run a business in defiance of moral principles, disaster, of one kind or another, is inevitable. The permanently prosperous men in any community are not its tricksters and deceivers, but its reliable and upright men. The Quakers are acknowledged to be the most upright men in the British community, and, although their numbers are small, they are the most prosperous. The Jains in India are similar both in numbers and sterling worth, and they are the most prosperous people in India.

Men speak of "building up a business," and, indeed, a business is as much a building as is a brick house or a stone church, albeit the process of building is a mental one. Prosperity, like a house, is a roof over a man's head, affording him protection and comfort. A roof presupposes a support, and a support necessitates a foundation. The roof of prosperity, then, is supported by the following eight pillars which are cemented in a foundation of moral consistency:-

1. Energy
2. Economy
3. Integrity
4. System
5. Sympathy
6. Sincerity
7. Impartiality
8. Self-reliance

A business built up on the faultless practice of all these principles would be so firm and enduring as to be invincible. Nothing could injure it; nothing could undermine its prosperity, nothing could interrupt its success, or bring it to the ground; but that success would be assured with incessant increase so long as the principles were adhered to. On the other hand, where these principles were all absent, there could be no success of any kind; there could not even be a business at all, for there would be nothing to produce the adherence of one part with another; but there would be that lack of life, that absence of fibre and consistency which animates and gives body and form to anything whatsoever. Picture a man with all these principles absent from his mind, his daily life, and even if your knowledge of these principles is but slight and imperfect, yet you could not think of such a man as doing any successful work. You could picture him as leading the confused life of a shiftless tramp but to imagine him at the head of a business, as the centre of an organisation, or as a responsible and controlling agent in any department of life – this you could not do, because you realise its impossibility. The fact that no one of moderate morality and intelligence can think of such a man as commanding any success, should, to all those who have not yet grasped the import of these principles, and therefore declare that morality is not a factor, but rather a hindrance, in prosperity, be a sound proof to them that their conclusion is totally wrong, for if it was right, then the greater the lack of these moral principles, the greater would be the success.

These eight principles, then, in greater or lesser degree, are the causative factors in all success of whatsoever kind. Underneath all prosperity they are the strong supports, and, howsoever appearances may be against such a conclusion, a measure of them informs and sustains every effort which is crowned with that excellence which men name success.

It is true that comparatively few successful men practice, in their entirety and perfection, all these eight principles, but there are those who do, and they are the leaders, teachers, and guides of men, the supports of human society, and the strong pioneers in the van of human evolution.

But while few achieve that moral perfection which ensures the acme of success, all lesser successes come from the partial observance of these principles which are so powerful in the production of good results that even perfection in any two or three of them alone is sufficient to ensure an ordinary degree of prosperity, and maintain a measure of local influence at least for a time, while the same perfection in two or three with partial excellence in all, or nearly all, the others, will render permanent that limited success and influence which will, necessarily, grow and extend in exact ratio with a more intimate knowledge and practice of those principles which, at present, are only partially incorporated in the character.

The boundary lines of a man's morality mark the limits of his success. So true is this that to know a man's moral status would be to know – to mathematically gauge – his ultimate success or failure. The temple of prosperity only stands in so far as it is supported by its moral pillars; as they are weakened, it becomes insecure; in so far as they are withdrawn, it crumbles away and totters to ruin.

Ultimate failure and defeat are inevitable where moral principles are ignored or defied – inevitable in the nature of things as cause and effect. As a stone thrown upward returns to the earth, so every deed, good or bad, returns upon him that sent it forth. Every unmoral or immoral act frustrates the end at which it aims, and every such succeeding act puts it further and further away as an achieved realisation. On the other hand, every moral act is another solid brick in the temple of prosperity, another round of strength and sculptured beauty in the pillars which support it.

Individuals, families, nations grow and prosper in harmony with their growth in moral strength and knowledge; they fall and fail in accordance with their moral decadence.

Mentally, as physically, only that which has form and solidity can stand and endure. The unmoral is nothingness, and from it nothing can be formed. It is the negation of substance. The immoral is destruction. It is the negation of form. It is a process of spiritual denudation. While it undermines and disintegrates, it leaves the scattered material ready for the wise builder to put it into form again; and the wise builder is Morality. The moral is substance, form, and building power in one. Morality always builds up and preserves, for that is its nature, being the opposite of immorality, which always breaks down and destroys. Morality is the master–builder everywhere, whether in individuals or nations.

Morality is invincible, and he who stands upon it to the end, stands upon an impregnable rock, so that his defeat is impossible, his triumph certain. He will be tried, and that to the uttermost, for without fighting there can be no victory, and so only can his moral powers be perfected, and it is in the nature of fixed principles, as of everything finely and perfectly wrought, to have their strength tested and proved. The steel bars which are to perform the strongest and best uses in the world must be subjected to a severe strain by the ironmaster, as a test of their texture and efficiency, before they are sent from his foundry. The brickmaker throws aside the bricks which have given way under the severe heat. So he who is to be greatly and permanently successful will pass through the strain of adverse circumstances and the fire of temptation with his moral nature not merely not undermined, but strengthened and beautified. He will be like a bar of well-wrought steel, fit for the highest use, and the universe will see, as the ironmaster his finely-wrought steel, that the use does not escape him.

Immorality is assailable at every point, and he who tries to stand upon it, sinks into the morass of desolation. Even while his efforts seem to stand, they are crumbling away. The climax of failure is inevitable. While the immoral man is chuckling over his ill-gotten gains, there is already a hole in his pocket through which his gold is falling. While he who begins with morality, yet deserts it for gain in the hour of trial, is like the brick which breaks on the first application of heat; he is not fit for use, and the universe casts him aside, yet not finally, for he is a being, and not a brick; and he can live and learn, can repent and be restored.

Moral force is the life of all success, and the sustaining element in all prosperity; but there are various kinds of success, and it is frequently necessary that a man should fail in one direction that he may reach up to a greater and more far-reaching success. If, for instance, a literary, artistic, or spiritual genius should begin by trying to make money, it may be, and often is, to his advantage and the betterment of his genius that he should fail therein, so that he may achieve that more sublime success wherein lies his real power. Many a millionaire would doubtless be willing to barter his millions for the literary success of a Shakespeare or the spiritual success of a Buddha, and would thereby consider that he had made a good bargain. Exceptional spiritual success is rarely accompanied with riches, yet financial success cannot in any way compare with it in greatness and grandeur. But I am not, in this book, dealing with the success of the saint or spiritual genius but with that success which concerns the welfare, well-being, and happiness of the broadly average man and woman, in a word, with the prosperity which, while being more or less connected with money – being present and temporal – yet is not confined thereto, but extends to and embraces all human activities, and which particularly relates to that harmony of the individual with his circumstances which produces that satisfaction called happiness and that comfort known as prosperity. To the achievement of this end, so desirable to the mass of mankind, let us now see how the eight principles operate, how the roof of prosperity is raised and made secure upon the pillars by which it is supported.

2. First pillar – Energy

Energy is the working power in all achievement. Inert coal it converts into fire, and water it transmutes into steam; it vivifies and intensifies the commonest talent until it approaches to genius, and when it touches the mind of the dullard, it turns into a living fire that which before was sleeping in inertia.

Energy is a moral virtue, its opposing vice being laziness. As a virtue, it can be cultivated, and the lazy man can become energetic by forcibly arousing himself to exertion. Compared with the energetic man, the lazy man is not half alive. Even while the latter is talking about the difficult of doing a thing, the former is doing it. the active man has done a considerable amount of work before the lazy man has roused himself from sleep. While the lazy man is waiting for an opportunity, the active man has gone out, and met and utilized half a dozen opportunities. He does things while the other is rubbing his eyes.

Energy is one of the primary forces: without it nothing can be accomplished. It is the basic element in all forms of action. The entire universe is a manifestation of tireless, though inscrutable energy. Energy is, indeed, life, and without it there would be no universe, no life. When a man has ceased to act, when the body lies inert, and all the functions have ceased to act, then we say he is dead; and in so far as a man fails to act, he is so far dead. Man, mentally and physically, is framed for action, and not for swinish ease. Every muscle of the body (being a lever for exertion) is a rebuke to the lazy man. Every bone and nerve is fashioned for resistance; every function and faculty is there for a legitimate use. All things have their end in action; all things are perfected in use.

This being so, there is no prosperity for the lazy man, no happiness, no refuge and no rest; for him, there is not even the ease which he covets, for he at last becomes a homeless outcast, a troubled, harried, despised man, so that the proverb wisely puts it that "The lazy man does the hardest work", in that, avoiding the systematic labour of skill, he brings upon himself the hardest lot.

Yet energy misapplied is better than no energy at all. This is powerfully put by St. John in the words: "I would have you either hot or cold; if you are lukewarm I will spew you out of my mouth". The extremes of heat and cold here symbolize the transforming agency of energy, in its good and bad aspects.

The lukewarm stage is colourless, lifeless, useless; it can scarcely be said to have either virtue or vice, and is merely barren empty, fruitless. The man who applies his abounding energy to bad ends, has, at the very power with which the strives to acquire his selfish ends, will bring upon him such difficulties, pains, and sorrows, that will compel him to learn by experience, and so at last to re-fashion his base of action. At the right moment, when his mental eyes open to better purposes, he will turn round and cut new and proper channels for the outflow of his power, and will then be just as strong in good as he formerly was in evil. This truth is beautifully crystallized in the old proverb, "The greater the sinner, the great the saint".

Energy is power, and without it there will be no accomplishment; there will not even be virtue, for virtue does not only consist of not doing evil, but also, primarily, of doing good. There are those who try, yet fail through insufficient energy. Their efforts are too feeble to produce positive results. Such are not vicious, and because they never do any deliberate harm, are usually spoken of as good men that fail. But to lack the initiative to do harm is not to be good; it is only to be weak and powerless. He is the truly good man who, having the power to do evil, yet chooses to direct his energies in ways that are good. Without a considerable degree of energy, therefore, there will be no moral power. What good there is, will be latent and sleeping; there will be no going forth of good, just as there can be no mechanical motion without the motive power.

Energy is the informing power in all doing in every department of life, and whether it be along material or spiritual lines. The call to action, which comes not only from the soldier but from the lips or pen of every teacher in every grade of thought, is a call to men to rouse their sleeping energy, and to do vigorously the task in hand. Even the men of contemplation and mediation never cease to rouse their disciples to exertion in meditative thought, is a call to men to rouse their sleeping energy, and to do vigorously the task in hand. Even the men of contemplation and meditation never cease to rouse their disciples to exertion in meditative thought. Energy is alike needed in all spheres of life, and not only are the rules of the soldier, the engineer and the merchant rules of action, but nearly all the percepts of the saviors, sages, and saints are precepts of doing.

The advice of one of the Great Teachers to his disciples – "Keep wide awake," tersely expresses the necessity for tireless energy if one's purpose is to be accomplished, and is equally good advice to the salesman as to the saint. "Eternal vigilance is the price of liberty," and liberty is the reaching of one's fixed end. It was the same Teacher that said: "If anything is to be done, let a man do it at once; let him attack it vigorously!" The wisdom of this advice is seen when it is remembered that action is creative, that increase and development follow upon legitimate use. To get more energy we must use to the full that which we already possess. Only to him that that is given. Only to him that puts his hand vigorously to some task does power and freedom come.

But energy, to be productive, must not only be directed towards good ends, it must be carefully controlled and conserved. "The conservation of energy" is a modern term expressive of that principle in nature by which no energy is wasted or lost, and the man whose energies are to be fruitful in results must work intelligently upon this principle. Noise and hurry are so much energy running to waste. "More haste, less speed". The maximum of noise usually accompanies the minimum of accomplishment. With much talk there is little doing. Working steam is not heard. It is the escaping steam which makes a great noise. It is the concentrated powder which drives the bullet to its mark.

In so far as a man intensifies his energies by conserving them, and concentrating them upon the accomplishment of his purpose, just so far does he gain quietness and silence, in response and calmness. It is great delusion that noise means power. There is no great baby than the blustering boaster. Physically a man, he is but an infant mentally, and having no strength to anything, and no work to show, he tries to make up for it by loudly proclaiming what he has done, or could do.

"Still waters run deep," and the great universal forces are inaudible. Where calmness is, there is the greatest power. Calmness is the sure indication of a strong, well-trained, patiently disciplined mind. The calm man knows his business, be sure of it. His words are few, but they tell. His schemes are well planned, and they work true, like a well-balanced machine. He sees a long way ahead, and makes straight for his object. The enemy, Difficulty, he converts into a friend, and makes profitable use of him, for he has studied well how to "agree with his adversary while he is in the way with him." Like a wise general, he has anticipated all emergencies. Indeed, he is the man who is prepared beforehand. In his meditations, in the counsels of his judgement, he has conferred with causes, and has caught the bent of all contingencies. He is never taken by surprise; is never in a hurry, is safe in the keeping of his own steadfastness, and is sure of his ground. You may think you have got him, only to find, the next moment, that you have tripped in your haste, and that he has got you, or rather that you, wanting calmness, have hurried yourself into the dilemma which you had prepared for him. Your impulse cannot do battle with his deliberation, but is foiled at the first attack; your uncurbed energy cannot turn aside the wisely directed steam of his concentrated power. He is "armed at all points." By a mental Ju-Jitsu acquired through self-discipline, he meets opposition in such a way that it destroys itself. Upbraid him with angry words, and the reproof hidden in his gentle reply searches to the very heart of your folly, and the fire of your anger sinks into the ashes of remorse. Approach him with a vulgar familiarity, and his look at once fill you with shame, and brings you back to your senses. As he is prepared for all events, so he is ready for all men; though no men are ready for him. All weaknesses are betrayed in his presence, and he commands by an inherent force which calmness has rendered habitual and unconscious.

Calmness, as distinguished from the dead placidity of languor, is the acme of concentrated energy. There is a focused mentality behind it. in agitation and excitement the mentality is dispersed. It is irresponsible, and is without force or weight. The fussy, peevish, irritable man has no influence. He repels, and not attracts. He wonders why his "easy going" neighbour succeeds, and is sought after, while he, who is always hurrying, worrying and troubling the miscalls it striving, falls and is avoided. His neighbour, being a calmer man, not more easy going but more deliberate, gets through more work, does it more skillfully, and is more self-possessed and manly.

This is the reason of his success and influence. His energy is controlled and used, while the other man's energy is dispersed and abused.

Energy, then, is the first pillar in the temple of prosperity, and without it, as the first and most essential equipment, there can be no prosperity. No energy means no capacity; there is no manly self-respect and independence. Amongst the unemployed will be found many who are unemployable through sheer lack of this first essential of work energy. The man that stands many hours a day at a street corner with his hands in his pockets and a pipe in his mouth, waiting for some one to treat him to a glass of beer, is little likely to find employment, or to accept it should it come to him. Physically flabby and mentally inert, he is every day becoming more some, is making himself more unfit to work, and therefore unfit to live. The energetic man may pass through temporary periods of unemployment and suffering, but it is impossible for him to become one of the permanently unemployed. He will either find work or make it, for inertia is painful to him, and work is a delight; and he who delights in work will not long remain unemployed.

The lazy man does not wish to be employed. He is in his element when doing nothing. His chief study is how to avoid exertion. To vegetate in semi torpor is his idea of happiness. He is unfit and unemployable. Even the extreme Socialist, who places all unemployment, at the door of the rich, would discharge a lazy, neglectful and unprofitable servant, and so add one more to the arm of the unemployed; for laziness is one of the lowest vices repulsive to all active, right minded men.

But energy is a composite power. It does not stand alone. Involved in it are qualities which go to the making of vigorous character and the production of prosperity. Mainly, these qualities are contained in the four following characteristics:-

1. Promptitude
2. Vigilance
3. Industry
4. Earnestness

The pillar of energy is therefore a concrete mass composed of these four tenacious elements. They are through, enduring, and are calculated to withstanding the wildest weather of adversity. They all make for life, power, capacity, and progress.

Promptitude is valuable possession. It begets reliability. People who are alert, prompt, and punctual are relied upon. They can be trusted to do their duty, and to do it vigorously and well. Masters who are prompt are a tonic to their employees, and a whip to those who are inclined to shirk. They are a means of wholesome discipline to those who would not otherwise discipline themselves. Thus while aiding their own usefulness and success, they contribute to the usefulness and success of others. The perfunctory worker, who is ever procrastinating, and is always behind time, becomes a nuisance, if not go himself, to others, and his services come to be regarded as of little economic value. Deliberation and dispatch, handmaids of promptitude, are valuable aids in the achievement of prosperity. In ordinary business channels, alacrity is a saving power, and promptness spells profit. It is doubtful whether a confirmed procrastinator ever succeeded in business. I have not yet met one such, though I have known many who have failed.

Vigilance is the guard of all the faculties and powers of the mind. It is the detective that prevents the entrance of any violent and destructive element. It is the close companion and protector of all success, liberty, and wisdom. Without this watchful attitude of mind, a man is a fool, and there is no prosperity for a fool. The fool allows his mind to be ransacked and robbed of its gravity, serenity, and judgement by mean thoughts and violent passions as they come along to molest him. He is never on his guard, but leaves open the doors of his mind to every nefarious intruder. He is so weak and unsteady as to be swept off his balance by every gust of impulse that overtakes him. He is an example to others of what they should not be. He is always a failure, for the fool is an offence to all men, and there is no society that can receive him with respect. As wisdom is the acme of strength, so folly is the other extreme of weakness.

The lack of vigilance is shown in thoughtlessness and in a general looseness in the common details of life. Thoughtlessness is built another name for folly. It lies at the root of a great deal of failure and misery. No one who aims at any kind of usefulness and prosperity (for usefulness in the body politic and prosperity to one's self cannot be served) can afford to be asleep with regard to his actions and the effect of those actions on other and reactively on himself. He must, at the outset of his career, wake up to a sense of his personal responsibility. He must know that wherever he is – in the home, the counting- house, the pulpit, the store, in the schoolroom or behind the counter, in company or alone, at work or at play - his conduct will materially affect his career for good or bad; for there is a subtle influence in behavior which leaves its impression on every man, woman, and child that it touches, and that impress is the determining factor in the attitude of persons towards one another. It is for this reason that the cultivation of good manners plays such an important part in all coherent society. If you carry about with you a disturbing or disagreeable mental defect, it needs not to be named and known to work its poison upon your affairs. Its corrosive influence will eat into all your efforts, and disfigure your happiness and prosperity, as powerful acid eats into and disfigures the finest steel. On the other hand, if you carry about an assuring and harmonious mental excellence, it needs no that those about you understand it to be influenced by it. They will be drawn towards you in good-will, often without knowing why, and that good quality will be the most powerful sport in all your affairs, bringing you friends and opportunities, and greatly aiding in the success of all your enterprises. It will even right your minor incapacities; covering a multitude of faults.

Thus we receive at the hands of the world according to the measure of our giving. For bad, bad; for good, good. For defective conduct, indifferent influence and imperfect success; for superior conduct lasting power and consummate achievement. We act, and the world responds. When the foolish man fails, he blames other, and sees no error in himself; but the wise man watches and corrects himself, and so is assured of success.

The man whose mind is vigilant and alert, has thereby a valuable equipment in the achievement of his aims; and if he be fully alive and wide-awake on all occasions, to all opportunities, and against all marring defects of character, what event, what circumstance, what enemy shall overtake him and find him unprepared? What shall prevent him from achieving the legitimate and at which he aims?

Industry brings cheerfulness and plenty. Vigorously industrious people are the happiest members of the community. They are not always the richest, if by riches is meant a superfluity of moncy; but they are always the most lighthearted and joyful, and the most satisfied with what they do and have, and are therefore the richer, if by richer we mean more abundantly blessed. Active people have no time for moping and brooding, or for dwelling selfishly upon their ailments and troubles. Things most used are kept the brightest, and people most employed best retain their brightness and buoyancy of spirit. Things unused tarnish quickest; and the time killer is attacked with ennui and morbid fancies. To talk of having to "kill time" is almost like a confession of imbecility; for who, in the short life at his disposal, and in a world so flooded with resources of knowledge with sound heads and good hearts can fill up every moment of every day usefully and happily, and if they refer to time at all, it is to the effect that it is all too short to enable them to do all that they would like to do.

Industry, too, promoted health and well-being. The active man goes to bed tired every night; his rest is sound and sweet, and he wakes up early in the morning, fresh and strong for another day's delightful toil. His appetite and digestion are good. He has an excellent sauce in recreation, and a good tonic in toil. What companionship can such a man have with moping and melancholy? Such morbid spirits hang around those who do little and dine excessively. People who make themselves useful to the community, receive back from the community their full share of health, happiness, and prosperity. They brighten the daily task, and keep the world moving. They are the gold of the nation and the salt of the earth.

"Earnestness," said a Great Teacher, "is the path of immortality. They who are in earnest do not die; they who are not in earnest are as if dead already." Earnestness is the dedication of the entire mind to its task. We live only in what we do. Earnest people are dissatisfied with anything short of the highest excellence in whatever they do, and they always reach that excellence. They are so many that are careless and half-hearted, so satisfied with a poor performance, that the earnest ones shine apart as it were, in their excellence. They are always plenty of "vacancies" in the ranks of usefulness and service for earnest people. There never was, and never will be, a deeply earnest man or woman who did not fill successfully some suitable sphere. Such people are scrupulous, conscientious, and painstaking, and cannot rest in ease until the very best is done, and the whole world is always on the lookout to reward the best. It always stands ready to pay the full price, whether in money, fame, friends, influence, happiness, scope or life, for that which is of surpassing excellence, whether it be in things material, intellectual, or spiritual. What ever you are – whether shopkeeper or saintly teacher you can safely give the very best to the world without any doubt or misgiving. If the indelible impress of your earnestness be on your goods in the one case, or on your words in the other, your business will flourish, or your precepts will live.

Earnest people make rapid progress both in their work and their character. It is thus that they live, and "do not die", for stagnation only is death, and where there is incessant progress and ever ascending excellence, stagnation and health are swallowed up in activity and life.

Thus is the making and masonry of the First pillar explained. He who builds it well, and sets it firm and straight, will have a powerful and enduring support in the business of his life.

3. Second pillar – Economy

It is said of Nature that she knows no vacuum. She also knows no waste. In the divine economy of Nature everything is conserved and turned to good account. Even excreta are chemically transmitted, and utilized in the building up of new forms. Nature destroys every foulness, not by annihilation, but by transmutation, by sweetening and purifying it, and making it serve the ends of things beautiful, useful and good.

That economy which, in nature is a universal principle, is in man a moral quality and it is that quality by which he preserves his energies, and sustains his place as a working unit in the scheme of things.

Financial economy is merely a fragment of this principle, or rather it is a material symbol of that economy which is purely mental, and its transmutations spiritual. The financial economist exchanges coppers for silver, silver for gold, gold for notes, and the notes he converts into the figures of a bank account. By these conversions of money into more readily transmissible forms he is the gainer in the financial management of his affairs. The spiritual economist transmutes passions into intelligence, intelligence into principles, principles into wisdom, and wisdom is manifested in actions which are few but of powerful effect. By all these transmutations he is the gainer in character and in the management of his life.

True economy is the middle way in all things, whether material or mental, between waste and undue retention. That which is wasted, whether money or mental energy, is rendered powerless; that which is selfishly retained and hoarded up, is equally powerless. To secure power, whether of capital or mentality, there must be concentration, but concentration must be followed by legitimate use. The gathering up of money or energy is only a means; the end is use; and it is use only that produces power.

An all round economy consists in finding the middle way in the following seven things:- Money, Food, Clothing, Recreation, Rest, Time and Energy.

Money is the symbol of exchange, and represents purchasing power. He who is anxious to acquire financial wealth as well as he who wishes to avoid debt – must study how to apportion, his expenditure in accordance with his income, so as to leave a margin of ever increasing working capital, or to have a little store ready in hand for any emergency. Money spent in thoughtless expenditure – in worthless pleasures or harmful luxuries – is money wasted and power destroyed; for, although a limited and subordinate power, the means and capacity for legitimate and virtuous purchase is, nevertheless, a power, and one that enters largely into the details of our everyday life. The spendthrift can never become rich, but if he begin with riches, must soon become poor. The miser, with all his stored-away gold, cannot be said to be rich, for he is in want, and his gold, lying idle, is deprived of its power of purchase. The thrifty and prudent are on the way to riches, for while they spend wisely they save carefully, and gradually enlarge their spheres as their growing means allow.

The poor man who is to become rich must begin at the bottom, and must not wish, nor try to appear affluent by attempting something far beyond his means. There is always plenty of room and scope at the bottom, and it is a safe place from which to begin, as there is nothing below, and everything above. Many a young businessman comes at once to grief by swagger and display which he foolishly imagines are necessary to success, but which, deceiving no one but himself, lead quickly to ruin. A modest and true beginning, in any sphere, will better ensure success than an exaggerated advertisement of one's standing and importance. The smaller the capital, the smaller should be the sphere of operations. Capital and scope are hand and glove, and they should fit. Concentrate your capital within the circle of its working power, and however circumscribed that circle may be it will continue to widen and extend as the gathering momentum of power presses for expression.

Above all take care always to avoid the two extremes of parsimony and prodigality.

Food represents life, vitality, and both physical and mental strength. There is a middle way in eating and drinking, as in all else. The man who is to achieve prosperity must be well nourished, but not overfed. The man that starves his body, whether through miserliness or asceticism (both forms of false economy), diminishes his mental energy, and renders his body too enfeebled to be the instrument for any strong achievement. Such a man courts sickly mindedness, a condition conducive only to failure.

The glutton, however, destroys himself by excess. His bestialized body becomes a stored up reservoir of poisons, which attract disease and corruption, while his mind becomes more and more brutalized and confused, and therefore more incapable. Gluttony is one of the lowest and most animal vices, and is obnoxious to all who pursue a moderate course.

The best workers and most successful men are they who are most moderate in eating and drinking. By taking enough nourishment, but not too much, they attain the maximum physical and mental fitness. Beings thus well-equipped by moderation, they are enabled to vigorously and joyfully fight the battle of life.

Clothing is covering and protection for the body, though it is frequently wrested from this economic purpose, and made a means of vain display. The two extremes to be avoided here are negligence and vanity. Custom cannot, and need not, be ignored; and cleanliness is all important. The ill-dressed, unkempt man or woman invites failure and loneliness. A man's dress should harmonize with his station in life, and it should be of good quality, and be well made and appropriate. Clothing should not be cast aside while comparatively new, but should be well worn. If a man be poor, he will not lose in either self-respect or the respect of others by wearing threadbare clothing if it be clean and his whole body be clean and neat. But vanity, leading to excessive luxury in clothing, is a vice which should be studiously avoided by virtuous people. I know a lady who had forty dresses in her wardrobe; also a man who had twenty walking-sticks, about the same number of hats, and some dozen mackintoshes; while another had some twenty or thirty pairs of boots. Rich people who thus squander money on piles of superfluous clothing, are courting poverty, for it is waste, and waste leads to want. The money so heedlessly spent could be better used, for suffering abounds and charity is noble.

An obtrusive display in clothing and jewellery bespeaks a vulgar and empty mind. Modest and cultured people are modest and becoming in their dress, and their spare money is wisely used in further enhancing their culture and virtue. Education and progress are of more importance to them than vain and needless apparel; and literature, art, and science are encouraged thereby. A true refinement is in the mind and behaviour, and a mind adorned with virtue and intelligence cannot add to its attractiveness though it may detract from it) by an ostentatious display of the body. Time spent in uselessly adorning the body could be more fruitfully employed. Simplicity in dress, as in other things, is the best. It touches the point of excellence in usefulness, comfort, and bodily grace, and bespeaks true taste and cultivated refinement.

Recreation is one of the necessities of life. Every man and women should have some definitive work as the main object of life, and to which a considerable amount of time should be devoted, and he should only turn from it at given and limited periods for recreation and rest. The object of recreation is greater buoyancy of both body and mind, with an increase of power in one's serious work. It is, therefore, a means, not an end; and this should ever be born in mind, for, to many, some forms of recreation innocent and good in themselves – become so fascinating that they are in danger of making them the end of life, and of thus abandoning duty for pleasure. To make of life a ceaseless round of games and pleasures, with no other object in life, is to turn living upside down, as it were, and it produces monotony and enervation. People who do it are the most unhappy of mortals, and suffer from languor, ennui, and peevishness. As sauce is an aid to digestion, and can only lead to misery when made the work of life. When a man has done his day's duty he can turn to his recreation with a free mind and a light heart, and both his work and his pleasure will be to him a source of happiness.

It is a true economy in this particular neither to devote the whole of one's time to work nor to recreation, but to apportion to each its time and place; and so fill out life with those changes which are necessary to a long life and a fruitful existence.

All agreeable changes is recreation and the mental worker will gain both in the quality and, quantity of his work by laying it down at the time appointed for restful and refreshing recreation; while the physical worker will improve in every way by turning to some form of study as a hobby or means of education.

As we do not spend all our time in eating or sleeping or resting, neither should we spend it in exercise or pleasure, but should give recreation its proper place as a natural tonic in the economic scheme of our life.

Rest is for recuperation after toil. Every self-respecting human being should do sufficient work every day to make his sleep restful and sweet, and his rising up fresh and bright.

Enough sleep should be taken, but not too much, over indulgence on the one hand, or deprivation on the other, are both harmful. It is an easy matter to find out how much sleep one requires. By going to bed early, and getting up early (rising a little earlier every morning if one has been in the habit of spending long hours in bed), one can very soon accurately gauge and adjust the number of hours he or she requires for complete recuperation. It will be found as the sleeping hours are shortened that the sleep becomes more and more sound and sweet, and the waking up more and more alert and bright. People who are to prosper in their work must not give way to ignoble ease and over indulgence in sleep. Fruitful labour, and not ease, is the true end of life, and ease is only good in so far as it subserves the ends of work. Sloth and prosperity can never be companions can never even approach each other. The sluggard will never overtake success, but failure will speedily catch up with him, and leave him defeated. Rest is to fit us for greater labour, and not to pamper us in indolence. When the bodily vigour is restored, the end of rest is accomplished. A perfect balance between labour and rest contributes considerably to health, happiness, and prosperity.

Time is that which we all possess in equal measure. The day is not lengthened for any man. We should therefore see to it that we do not squander its precious minutes in unprofitable waste. He who spends his time in self-indulgence and the pursuit of pleasure, presently finds himself old, and nothing has been accomplished. He who fills full with useful pursuits the minutes as they come and go, grows old in honour and wisdom, and prosperity abides with him. Money wasted can be restored; health wasted can be restored; but time wasted can never be restored.

It is an old saying that "time is money." It is, in the same way, health, and strength, and talent, and genius, and wisdom, in accordance with the manner in which it is used; and to properly use it, the minutes must be seized upon as they come, for once they are past they can never be recalled. The day should be divided into portions, and everything – work, leisure, meals, recreation – should be attend to in its proper time; and the time of preparation should not be overlooked or ignored. Whatever a man does, he will do it better and more successfully by utilizing some small portion of the day in preparing his mind for his work. The man who gets up early in order to think and plan, that he may weigh and consider and forecast, will always manifest greater skill and success in his particular pursuit, than the man who lives in bed till the last moment, and only gets up just in time to begin breakfast. An hour spend in this way before breakfast will prove of the greatest value in making one's efforts fruitful. It is a means of calming and clarifying the mind, and of focussing one's energies so as to render them more powerful and effective. The best and most abiding success is that which is made before eight o'clock in the morning. He who is at his business at six o'clock, will always other conditions being equal be a long way ahead of the man who is in bed at eight. The lie a bed heavily handicaps himself in the race of life. He gives his early-rising competitor two or three hours start every day. How can he ever hope to win with such a self-imposed tax upon his time? At the end of a year that two or three hours start every day is shown in a success which is the synthesis of accumulated results. What, then, must be the difference between the efforts of these two men at the end, say, of twenty years! The lie-a-bed, too, after he gets up is always in a hurry trying to regain lost time, which results in more loss of time, for hurry always defeats its own end. The early rise, who thus economies his time, has no need to hurry, for he is always ahead of the hour, is always well up with his work; he can well afford to be calm and deliberate, and to do carefully and well whatever is in hand, for his good habit shows itself at the end of the day in the form of a happy frame of mind, and in bigger results in the shape of work skillfully and successfully done.

In the economizing of time, too, there will be many things which a man will have to eliminate from his life; some of things and pursuits which he loves, and desires to retain, will have to be sacrifice to the main purpose of his life. The studied elimination of non-essentials from one's daily life is a vital factor in all great achievement. All great men are adepts in this branch of economy, and it plays an important part in the making of their greatness. It is a form of economy which also enters into the mind, the actions, and the speech, eliminating from them all that is superfluous, and that impedes, and does not sub-serve, the end aimed at. Foolish and unsuccessful people talk carelessly and aimlessly, act carelessly and aimlessly, and allow everything that comes along good, bad, and different to lodge in their mind.

The mind of the true economist is a sieve which lets everything fall through except that which is of use to him in the business of his life. He also employs only necessary words, and does only necessary actions, thus vastly minimizing friction and waste of power.

To go to bed betime and to get up betime, to fill in every working minute with purposeful thought and effective action, this is the true economy of time.

Energy is economized by the formation of good habits. All vices are a reckless expenditure of energy. Sufficient energy is thoughtlessly wasted in bad habits to enable men to accomplish the greatest success, if conserved and used in right directions. If economy be practiced in the six points already considered, much will be done in the conservation of one's energies, but a man must go still further, and carefully husband his vitality by the avoidance of all forms of physical self-indulgences and impurities, but also all those mental vices such as hurry, worry, excitement, despondency, anger, complaining and envy – which deplete the mind and render it unfit for any important work or admirable achievement. They are common forms of mental dissipation which a man of character should study how to avoid and overcome. The energy wasted in frequent fits of bad temper would, if controlled and properly directed, give a man strength of mind, force of character, and much power to achieve. The angry man is a strong man made weak by the dissipation of his mental energy. He needs self-control to manifest his strength. The calm man is always his superior in any department of life, and will always take precedence of him, both in his success, and in the estimation of others. No man can afford to disperse his energies in fostering bad habits and bad tendencies of mind. Every vice, however, apparently small will tell against him in the battle of life. Every harmful self-indulgence will come back to him in the form of some trouble or weakness. Every moment of riot or of pandering to his lower inclinations will make his progress more laborious, and will hold him back from scaling the high heaven of his wishes for achievement. On the other hand, he who economizes his energies, and bends them towards the main task of his life, will make rapid progress, and nothing will prevent him from reaching the golden city of success.

It will be seen that economy is something far more profound and far reaching than the mere saving of money. It touches every part of our nature and every phase of our life. The old saying, "Take care of the pence, and the pounds will take care of themselves", may be regarded as a parable, for the lower passions as native energy; it is the abuse of that energy that is bad, and if this personal energy be taken care of and stored up and transmuted, it reappears as force of character. To waste this valuable energy in the pursuit of vice is like wasting the pence, and so losing the pounds, but to take care of it for good uses is to store up the pence of passions, and so gain the golden pounds of good. Take care, therefore, of the lower energies, and the higher achievements will take care of themselves.

The Pillar of Economy, when soundly built, will be found to be composed largely of these four qualities:-

1. Moderation
2. Efficiency
3. Resourcefulness
4. Originality

Moderation is the strong core of economy. It avoids extremes, finding the middle way in all things. It also consists in abstaining from the unnecessary and the harmful. There can be no such things as moderation in that which is evil, for that would be excess. A true moderation abstains from evil. It is not a moderate use of fire to put our hands into it, but to warm them by it at a safe distance. Evil is a fire that will burn a man though he but touch it; a harmful luxury is best left severely alone. Smoking, snuff taking, alcoholic drinking, gambling, and other such common vices, although they have dragged thousands down to ill health, misery, and failure, have never helped one towards health, happiness and success. The man who eschews them will always be ahead of the man that pursues them, their talents and opportunities being equal. Healthy, happy, and long lived people are always moderate and abstemious in their habits. By moderation the life forces are preserved; by excess they are destroyed. Men, also, who carry moderation into their thoughts, allaying their passions and feelings, avoiding all unwholesome extremes and morbid sensations and sentiments, add knowledge and wisdom to happiness and health, and thereby attain to the highest felicity and power. The immoderate destroy themselves by their own folly. They weaken their energies and stultify their capabilities, and instead of achieving an abiding success, reach only, at best, a fitful and precarious prosperity.

Efficiency proceeds from the right conservation of one's forces and powers. All skill is the use of concentrated energy. Superior skill, as talent and genius, is a higher degree of concentrated force. Men are always skillful in that which they love, because the mind is almost ceaselessly centered upon it. Skill is the result of that mental economy which transmutes thought into invention and action. There will be no prosperity without skill, and one's prosperity will be in the measure of one's skill. By a process of natural selection, the inefficient fall in to their right places. Among the badly paid or unemployed; for who will employ a man who cannot, or will not, do his work properly? An employer may occasionally keep such a man out of charity; but this will be exceptional; as places of business, offices, households, and all centers of organized activity, are not charitable institutions, but industrial bodies which stand or fall but the fitness and efficiency of their individual members.

Skill is gained by thoughtfulness and attention. Aimless and inattentive people are usually out of employment – to wit, the lounger at the street corner. They cannot do the simplest thing properly, because they will not rouse up the mind to thought and attention. Recently an acquaintance of mine employed a tramp to clean his windows, but the man had refrained from work and systematic thought for so long that he had become incapable of both, and could not even clean a window. Even when shown how to do it, he could not follow the simple instructions given. This is an instance, too, of the fact that the simplest thing requires a measure of skill in the doing. Efficiency largely determines a man's place among his fellows, and leads one on by steps to higher and higher positions as greater powers are developed. The good workman is skillful, with his tools, while the good man is skillful with his thoughts. Wisdom is the highest form of skill. Aptitude is incipient wisdom. There is one right way of doing everything, even the smallest, and a thousand wrong ways. Skill consists in finding the one right way, and adhering to it. The inefficient bungle confusedly about among the thousand wrong ways, and do not adopt the right even when it is pointed out to them. They do this in some cases because they think, in their ignorance, that they know best, thereby placing themselves in a position where it becomes impossible to learn, even though it be only to learn how to clean a window or sweep a floor. Thoughtlessness and inefficiency are all too common. There is plenty of room in the world for common. There is plenty of room in the world for thoughtful and efficient people. Employers of labour know how difficult it is to get the best workmanship. The good workman, whether with tools or brain, whether with speech or thought, will always find a place for the exercise of his skill.

Resourcefulness is the outcome of efficiency. It is an important element in prosperity, for the resourceful man is never confounded. He may have many falls, but he will always be equal to the occasion, and will be on his feet again immediately. Resourcefulness has its fundamental cause in the conservation of energy. It is energy transmuted. When a man cuts off certain mental or bodily vices which have been depleting him of his energy, what becomes of the energy so conserved? It is not destroyed or lost, for energy can never be destroyed or lost. It becomes productive energy. It reappears in the form of fruitful thought. The virtuous man is always more successful than the vicious man because he is teeming with resources. His entire mentality is alive and vigorous, abounding with stored up energy. What the vicious man wastes in barren indulgence, the virtuous man uses in fruitful industry. A new life and a new world, abounding with all fascinating pursuits and pure delights, open up to the man who shuts himself off from the old world of animal vice, and his place will be assured by the resources which will well up within him. Barren seed perishes in the earth; there is no place for it in the fruitful economy of nature. Barren minds sink in the struggle of life. Human society makes for good, and there is no room in it for the emptiness engendered by vice. But the barren mind will not sink for ever. When it wills, it can become fruitful and regain itself. By the very nature of existence, by the eternal law of progress, the vicious man must fall; but having fallen, he can rise again. He can turn from vice to virtue, and stand, self-respecting and secure, upon his own resources.

The resourceful men invent, discover, initiate. They cannot fail, for they are in the stream of progress. They are full of new schemes, new methods, new hopes, and their life is so much fuller and richer thereby. They are men of supple minds. When a man fails to improve his business, his work, his methods, he falls out of the line of progress, and has begun to fail. His mind has become stiff and inert like the body of an aged man, and so fails to keep pace with the rapidly moving ideas and plans of resourceful minds. A resourceful mind is like a river which never runs dry, and which affords refreshment, and supplies new vigour, in times of drought. Men of resources are men of new ideas, and men of new ideas flourish where others fade and decay.

Originality is resourcefulness ripened and perfected. Where there is originality there is genius, and men of genius are the lights of the world. Whatever work a man does, he should fall back upon his own resources in the doing it. While learning from others, he should not slavishly imitate them, but should put himself into his work, and so make it new and original. Original men get the ear of the world. They may be neglected at first, but they are always ultimately accepted, and become patterns for mankind. Once a man has acquired the knack of originality, he takes his place as a leader among men in his particular department of knowledge and skill. But originality cannot be forced; it can only be developed; and it is developed by proceeding from excellence to excellence, by ascending in the scale of skill by the full and right use of one's mental powers. Let a man consecrate himself to his work, let him, so consecrated, concentrate all his energies upon it, and the day will come when the world will hail him as one of its strong sons; and he, too, like Balzac who, after many years of strenuous toil, one day exclaimed, "I am about to become a genius!, "I am about to become a genius" will at least discover, to his joy, that he has joined the company of original minds, the gods who lead mankind into newer, higher, and more beneficent ways.

The composition of the Second Pillar is thus revealed. Its building awaits the ready work man who will skillfully apply his mental energies.

4. Third pillar – Integrity

There is no striking a cheap bargain with prosperity. It must be purchased, not only with intelligent labor, but with moral force. as the bubble cannot endure, so the fraud cannot prosper. He makes a feverish spurt in the acquirement of money, and then collapses. Nothing is ever gained, ever can be gained, by fraud. It is but wrested for a time, to be again returned with heavy interest. But fraud is not confined to the unscrupulous swindler. All who are getting, or trying to get, money without giving an equivalent are practicing fraud, whether they know it or not. Men who are anxiously scheming how to get money without working for it, are frauds, and mentally they are closely allied to the thief and swindler under whose influence they come, sooner or later, and who deprives them of their capital. What is a thief but a man who carries to its logical or later, and who deprives them of their capital. What is a thief but a man who carries to its logical extreme the desire to possess without giving a just return – that is, unlawfully? The man that courts prosperity must, in all his transactions, whether material or mental, study how to give a just return for that which he receives. This is the great fundamental principle in all sound commerce, while in spiritual things it becomes the doing to others that which we would have them do to us, and applied to the forces of the universe, it is scientifically stated in the formula, "Action and Reaction are equal."

Human life is reciprocal, not rapacious, and the man who regards all others as his legitimate prey will soon find himself stranded in the desert of ruin, far away from the path of prosperity. He is too far behind in the process of evolution to cope successfully with honest man. The fittest, the best, always survive, and he being the worst, cannot therefore continue. His end, unless the change in time, is sure it is the goal, the filthy hovel, or the place of the deserted outcast. His efforts are destructive, and not constructive, and he thereby destroys himself.

It was Carlyle who, referring to Mohammed being then universally regarded by Christians as an impostor, exclaimed, "An impostor found a religion! An impostor couldn't built a brick house" an impostor, a liar a cheat the man of dishonesty cannot build as he has neither tools or material with which to build. He can no more build up a business, a character, a career, a success, than he can found a religion or build a brick house. He not only does not build, but all his energies are bent on undermining what others have built, but his being impossible, he undermines himself.

Without integrity, energy and economy will at last fail, but aided by integrity, their strength will be greatly augmented. There is not an occasion in life in which the moral factor does not play an important part. Sterling integrity tell wherever it is, and stamps it hall mark on all transactions; and it does this because of its wonderful coherence and consistency, and its invincible strength. For the man of integrity is in line with the fixed laws of things – not only with the fundamental principles on which human society rests, but with the laws which hold the vast universe together. Who shall set these at naught? Who, then, shall undermine the man of unblemished integrity? He is like a strong tree whose roots are fed by perennial springs, and which no tempest can law low.

To be complete and strong, integrity must embrace the whole man, and extend to all the details of his life; and it must be so through and permanent as to withstand all temptations to swerve into compromise. To fail in one point is to fail in all, and to admit, under stress, a compromise with falsehood, howsoever necessary and insignificant it may appear, is to throw down the shield of integrity, and to stand exposed to the onslaughts of evil.

The man who works as carefully and conscientiously when his employer is away as when his eye is upon him, will not long remain in an inferior position. Such integrity in duty, in performing the details of his work, will quickly lead him into the fertile regions of prosperity.

The shirker, on the other hand – he who does not scruple to neglect his work when his employer is not about, thereby robbing his employer of the time and labour for which he is paid – will quickly come to the barren region of unemployment, and will look in vain for needful labour.

There will come a time, too, to the man who is not deeply rooted in integrity, when it will seem necessary to his prospects and prosperity that he should tell a lie or do a dishonest thing – I say, to the man who is not deeply rooted in this principle, for a man of fixed and enlightened integrity knows that lying and dishonesty can never under any circumstance be necessary, and therefore he neither needs to be tempted in this particular, nor can he possibly be tempted but the one so tempted must be able to cast aside the subtle insinuation of falsehood which, in a time of indecision and perplexity, arises within him, and he must stand firmly by the principle, being willing to lose and suffer rather than sink into obliquity. In this way only can he become enlightened concerning this moral principle, and discover the glad truth that integrity does not lead to loss and suffering, but to gain and joy; that honesty and deprivation are not, and cannot be, related as cause and effect.

It is this willingness to sacrifice rather than be untrue that leads to enlightenment in all spheres of life; and the man who, rather than sacrifice some selfish aim, will lie or deceive, has forfeited his right to moral enlightenment, and takes his place lower down among the devotees of deceit, among the doers of shady transactions, than men of no character and no reputation.

A man is not truly armoured with integrity until he has become incapable of lying or deceiving either by gesture, word, or act; until he sees, clearly, openly, and freed from all doubt, the deadly effects of such moral turpitude. The man so enlightened is protect from all quarters, and can no more be undermined by dishonest men than the sun can be pulled down from heaven by madmen, and the arrows of selfishness and treachery that may be poured upon him will rebound from the strong armour of his integrity and the bright shield of his righteousness, leaving him unharmed and untouched.

A lying tradesman will tell you that no man can thrive and be honest in these days of keen competition. How can such a man know this, seeing that he has never tried honest? Moreover, such a man has no knowledge of honesty, and his statement is therefore, a statement of ignorance, and ignorance and falsehood so blind a man that he foolishly imagines all are as ignorant and false as himself. I have known such tradesmen, and have seen them come to ruin. I once heard a businessman make the following statement in a public meeting:-"No man can be entirely honest in business; he can only be approximately honest." He imagined that his statement revealed the condition of the business world; it did not, it revealed his own condition. He was merely telling his audience that he was a dishonest man, but his ignorance, moral ignorance, prevented him from seeing this. Approximate honesty is only another term for dishonesty. The man who deviated a little from the straight path, will deviate more. He has no fixed principle of right and is only thinking of his own advantage. That he persuades himself that his particular dishonesty is of a white and harmless kind, and that he is not so bad as his neighbour, is only of the many forms of self-delusion which ignorance of moral principles creates.

Right doing between man and main in the varied relations and transactions of life is the very soul of integrity. It includes, but is more than, honesty. It is the backbone of human society, and the support of human institutions. Without it there would be no trust, no confidence between men, and the business world would topple to its fall.

As the liar thinks all men are liars, and treats them as such, so the man of integrity treats all men with confidence. He trusts them, and they trust him. His clear eye and open hand shame the creeping fraud so that he cannot practice his fraud on him. As Emerson has so finely put it – "Trust men and they will be true to you, even though they make an exception in your favor to all their rules of trade."

The upright man by his very presence commands the morality of those about him making them better than they were. Men are powerfully influenced by one another, and, as good is more powerful than evil, the strong and good man both shames and elevates, by his contact, the weak and bad.

The man of integrity carries about with him an unconscious grandeur which both awes and inspires. Having lifted himself above the petty, the mean, and the false, those coward vices slink from his presence in confusion. The highest intellectual gift cannot compare with this lofty moral grandeur. In the memory of men and the estimation of the world the man of integrity occupies a higher place than the man of genius. Buckminster says, "The moral grandeur of an independent integrity is the sublimest thing in nature." It is the quality in man which produces heroes. The man of unswerving rectitude is, intrinsically, always a hero. It only needs the occasion to bring out the heroic element. He is always, too, possessed a permanent happiness. The man of genius may be very unhappy, but not to the man of integrity. Nothing nor sickness, nor calamity, nor death – can deprive him of that permanent satisfaction which inheres in uprightness.

Rectitude leads straight to prosperity by four successive steps. First, the upright man wins the confidence of others. Second, having gained their confidence, they put trust in him. Third, this trust, never being violated, produces a good reputation; and fourth, a good reputation spreads further and further, and so bring about success.

Dishonesty has the reverse effect. By destroying the confidence of others, it produces in them suspicion and mistrust, and these bring about a bad reputation, which culminates in failure.

The Pillar of Integrity is held together by these four virile elements:

1. Honesty
2. Fearlessness
3. Purposefulness
4. Invincibility

Honesty is the surest way to success. The day at last comes when the dishonest man repents in sorrow and suffering: but not man ever needs to repent of having been honest. Even when the honest man fails – as he does sometimes, through lacking other of these pillars, such as energy, economy, or system his failure is not the grievous thing it is to the dishonest man, for he can always rejoice in the fact that he has never defrauded a fellow being. Even in his darkest hour he finds repose in a clear conscience.

Ignorant men imagine that dishonesty is a short cut to prosperity. This is why they practice it. The dishonest man is morally short sighted. Like the drunkard who sees the immediate pleasure of his habit, but not the ultimate degradation, he sees the immediate effect of a dishonest act – a larger profit but not its ultimate outcome; he does not see that an accumulated number of such acts must inevitably undermine his character, and bring his business toppling about his ears in ruin. While pocketing his gains, and thinking how cleverly and successfully he is imposing on others, he is all the time imposing on himself, and every coin thus gained must be paid back with added interest, and from this just retribution there is no possible loophole of escape. This moral gravitation is an sure and unvarying as the physical gravitation of a stone to the earth.

The tradesman who demands of his assistants that they shall be, and misrepresents his goods to customers, is surrounding himself on all hands with suspicion, mistrust, and hatred. Even the moral weaklings who carry out his instructions, despise him while defiling themselves with his unclean work. How can success thrive in such a poisonous atmosphere? The spirit of ruin is already in such a business, and the day of his fall is ordained.

An honest man may fail, but not because he is honest, and his failure will be honourable, and will not injure his character and reputation. His failure, too, resulting doubtless from his incapacity in the particular direction of his failure, will be a means of leading him into something more suited to his talents, and thus to ultimate success.

Fearlessness accompanies honesty. The honest man has a clear eye and an unflinching gaze. He looks his fellow men in the face, and his speech is direct and convincing. The liar and cheat hangs his head; his eye is muddy and his gaze oblique. He cannot look another man in the eye, and his speech arouses mistrust, for it is ambiguous and unconvincing.

When a man has fulfilled his obligations, he has nothing to fear. All his business relations are safe and secure. His methods and actions will endure the light of day. Should he pass through a difficult time, and, get into debt, everybody will trust him and be willing to wait for payment, and all his debts will be paid. Dishonest people try to avoid paying their debts, and they live in fear; but the honest man tries to avoid getting into debt, but when debt overtakes him, he does not fear, but, redoubling his exertions, his debts are paid.

The dishonest are always in fear. They do not fear debt, but fear that they will have to pay their debts. They fear their fellow men, fear the established authorities, fear the results of all that they do, and they are in constant fear of their misdeeds being revealed, and of the consequences which may at any moment overtake them.

The honest man is rid of all this burden of fear. He is light hearted, and walks erect among his fellows; not assuming a part, and skulking and cringing, but being himself, and meeting eye to eye. Not deceiving or injuring any, there are none to fear, and anything and against him can only rebound to his advantage.

And this fearlessness is, in itself, a tower to strength in a man's life, supporting him through all emergencies, enabling him to battle manfully with difficulties, and in the end securing for him that success of which he cannot be dispossessed.

Purposefulness is the direct outcome of that strength of character which integrity fosters. The man of integrity is the man of direct aims and strong and intelligent purposes. He does not guess, and work in the dark. All his plans have in them some of that moral fiber of which his character is wrought. A man's work will always in some way reflect himself, and the man of sound integrity is the man of sound plan. He weights and considers and looks ahead, and so is less likely to make serious mistakes, or to bungle into a dilemma from which it is difficult to escape. Taking a moral view of all things, and always considering moral consequences, he stands on a firmer and more exalted ground than the man of mere policy and expedience; and while commanding a more extended view of any situation, he wields the greater power which a more comprehensive grasp of details with the principles involved, confers upon him. Morality always has the advantage of expediency. Its purposes always reach down far below the surface, and are therefore more firm and secure, more strong and lasting. There is a native directness, too, about integrity, which enables the man to get straight to the mark in whatever he does, and which makes failure almost impossible.

Strong men have strong purposes, and strong purposes lead to strong achievements. The man of integrity is above all men strong, and his strength is manifested in that thoroughness with which he does the business of his life; thoroughness which commands respect, admiration, and success.

Invincibility is a glorious protector, but it only envelopes the man whose integrity is perfectly pure and unassailable. Never to violate, even in the most insignificant particular, the principle of integrity, is to be invincible against all the assaults of innuendo, slander, and misrepresentation. The man who has failed in one point is vulnerable, and the shaft of evil, entering that point, will lay him low, like the arrow in the heel of Achilles. Pure and perfect integrity is proof against all attack and injury, enabling its possessor to meet all opposition and persecution with dauntless courage and sublime equanimity. No amount of talent, intellect, or business acumen can give a man that power of mind and peace of heart which come from an enlightened acceptance and observance of lofty moral principles. Moral force is the greatest power. Let the seeker for a true prosperity discover this force, let him foster and develop it in his mind and in his deeds, and as he succeeds he will take his place among the strong leaders of the earth.

Such is the strong and adamantine Pillar of integrity. Blessed and prosperous above all men will be he who builds its incorruptible masonry into the temple of his life.

5. Fourth pillar – System

System is that principle of order by which confusion is rendered impossible. In the natural and universal order everything is in its place, so that the vast universe runs more perfectly than the most perfect machine. Disorder in space would mean the destruction of the universe; and disorder in a man's affairs destroys his work and his prosperity.

All complex organizations are built up by system. No business or society can develop into large dimensions apart from system, and this principle is preeminently the instrument of the merchant, the businessman, and the organizer of institutions.

There are many departments in which a disorderly man may succeed – although attention to order would increase his success but he will not succeed in business unless he can place the business entirely in the hands of a systematic manager, who will thereby remedy his own defect.

All large business concerns have been evolved along definitely drawn systematic lines, any violation of which would be disastrous to the efficiency and welfare of the business. Complex business or other organizations are built up like complex bodies in nature, by scrupulous attention to details. The disorderly man thinks he can be careless about every thing but the main end, but by ignoring the means he frustrates the end. By the disarrangement of details, organisms perish, and by the careless neglect of details, the growth of any work or concern is prevented.

Disorderly people waste an enormous amount of time and energy. The time frittered away in hunting for things is sufficient, were if conserved by order, to enable them to achieve any success, for slovenly people never have a place for anything, and have to hunt, frequently for a long time, for any article which they require. In the irritation, bad humour, and chagrin which this daily hunting for things brings about, as much energy is dissipated as would be required to build up a big business, or scale the highest heights of achievement in any direction.

Orderly people conserve both their time and energy. They never lose anything, and therefore never have to find anything. Everything is in its place, and the hand can be at once placed upon it, though it be in the dark. They can well afford to be cool and deliberate and so use their mental energies in something more profitable than irritation, bad temper and accusing others for their own lack of order.

There is a kind of genius in system which can perform apparent wonders with ease. A systematic man can get through so great a quantity of work in such a short time, and with such freedom from such exhaustion, as to appear almost miraculous. He scales the heights of success while his slovenly competitor is wallowing hopelessly in the bogs of confusion. His strict observance of the law of order enables him to reach his ends, swiftly and smoothly, without friction or loss of time.

The demands of system, in all departments of the business world, are as rigid and exacting as the holy vows of a saint, and cannot be violated in the smallest particular but at the risk of one's financial prospects. In the financial world, the law of order is an iron necessity, and he who faultlessly observes it, saves time, temper, and money.

Every enduring achievement in human society rests upon a basis of system; so true is this, that were system withdrawn, progress would cease. Think, for instance, of the vast achievements of literature the works of classic authors and of great geniuses; the great poems, the innumerable prose works, the monumental histories, the soul – stirring orations; think also the social intercourse of human society, of it religions, its legal statutes, and its vast fund of book knowledge think of all these wonderful resources and achievements of language, and then reflect that they all depend for their origin, growth, and continuance on the systematic arrangements of twenty six letters, an arrangement having inexhaustible and illimitable results by the fact of its rigid limitation within certain fixed rules.

Again, all the wonderful achievements of mathematics have come from the systematic arrangement of ten figures; while the most complex piece of machinery, with its thousands of parts working together smoothly and almost noiselessly to the achievement of the end for which it was designed, was brought forth by the systematic observance of a few mechanical laws.

Herein we see how system simplifies that is complex: how it makes easy that which was difficult; how it relates an infinite variety of details of the one central law or order, and so enables them to be dealt with and accounted for with perfect regularity, and with an entire absence of confusion.

The scientist names and classifies the myriad details of the universe, from the microscopic rotifer to the telescopic star, by his observance of the principle of system, so that out of many millions of objects, reference can be made to any one object in, at most, a few minutes. It is this faculty of speedy references and swift dispatch which is of such overwhelming importance in every department of knowledge and industry, and the amount of time and labour thus saved to humanity is so vast as to be incompatible. We speak of religious, political, and business systems; and so on, indicating that all things in human society are welded together by the adhesive qualities of order.

System is, indeed, one of the great fundamental principles in progress, and in the binding together, in one complete whole, of the world's millions of human beings while they are at the same time each striving for a place and are competing with one another in opposing aims and interest.

We see here how system is allied with greatness, for the many separate units whose minds are untrained to the discipline of system, are kept in their places by the organizing power of the comparatively few who perceive the urgent, the inescapable, necessity for the establishment of fixed and inviolable rules, whether in business, law, religion, science, or politics in fact, in every sphere of human activity for immediately two human beings meet together, they need some common ground of understanding for the avoidance of confusion; in a word, some system to regulate their actions.

Life is too short for confusion; and knowledge grows and progress proceeds along avenues of system which prevent retardation and retrogression, so that he who systematizes his knowledge or business, simplifies and enhances it for his successor, enabling him to begin, with a free mind, where he left off.

Every large business has its system which renders its vast machinery workable, enabling it to run like a well-balanced and well-oiled machine. A remarkable business man, a friend of mine, once told me that he could have his huge business for twelve months, and it would run on without hitch till his return; and he does occasionally leave it for several months, while travelling, and on his return, every man, boy and girl; every tool, book, and machine; every detail down to the smallest, is in its place doing its work as when he left; and no trouble, no difficulty, no confusion has arisen.

There can be no marked success part from a love of regularity and discipline, and the avoidance of friction, along with the restfulness and efficiency of mind which spring from such regularity. People who abhor discipline, whose minds are ungoverned and anarchic, and who are careless and irregular in their thinking, their habits and the management of their affairs, cannot be highly successful and prosperous, and they fill their lives with numerous worries, troubles, difficulties, and petty annoyances, all of which would disappear under a proper regulation of their lives.

An unsystematic mind is an untrained mind and it can no more cope with well-disciplined minds in the race of life than an untrained athlete can successfully complete with a carefully trained competitor in athletic competitor in athletic races. The ill-disciplined mind, that thinks anything will do, rapidly falls behind the well-disciplined minds who are convinced that only the best will do in the strenuous race for the prizes of life, whether they be material, mental, or moral prizes. The man who, when he comes to do his work, is unable to find his tools, or to balance his figures, or to find the key of his desk, or the key to his thoughtless, will be struggling in his self-made toils while his methodical neighbor will be freely and joyfully scaling the invigorating heights of successful achievement. The business man whose method is slovenly, or cumbersome, or behind the most recent developments of skilled minds, should only blame himself as his prospects are decadent, and should wake up to the necessity for more highly specialized and effective methods in his concern. He should seize upon every thing – every invention and idea – that will enable him to economize time and labour, and aid him in thoroughness, deliberation and dispatch.

System is the law by which everything – every organism, business, character, nation, empire – is built. By adding cell to cell, department to department, thought to thought, law to law, and colony to colony in orderly sequence and classification, all things, concerns and institutions grow in magnitude, and evolve to completeness. The man who is continually improving his methods, is gaining in building power; it therefore behoves the business man to be resourceful and inventive in the improvement of his methods, for the builders – whether of cathedrals or characters, business or religions – are the strong ones of the earth, and the protectors and pioneers of humanity. The systematic builder is a creator and preserver, while the man of disorder demolishes and destroys, and no limit can be set to the growth of a man's powers, the completeness of his character, the influence of his organization, or the extent of his business, if he but preserve intact the discipline of order, and have every detail in its place, keep every department to its special task, and tabulate and classify with such efficiency and perfection as to enable him at any moment to bring under examination or into requisition to the remotest detail in connection with his special work.

In system is contained these four ingredients:

1. Readiness
2. Accuracy
3. Utility
4. Comprehensiveness

Readiness is aliveness. It is that spirit of alertness by which a situation is immediately grasped and dealt with. The observance of system fosters and develops this spirit. The successful General must have the power of readily meeting any new and unlooked for move on the part of the enemy; so every businessman must have the readiness to deal with any unexpected development affecting his line of trade; and so also must the man of thought be able to deal with the details of any new problems which may arise. Dilatoriness is a vice that is fatal to prosperity, for it leads to incapability and stupidity. The men of ready hands, ready hearts, and ready brains, who know what they are doing, and do it methodically, skillfully, and with smooth yet consummate despatch are the men who need to think little of prosperity as an end, for it comes to them whether they seek it or not; success runs after them, and knocks at their door; and they unconsciously command it by the superb excellence of their faculties and methods.

Accuracy is of supreme importance in all commercial concerns and enterprises, but there can be no accuracy apart from system, and a system which is more or less imperfect will involve its originator in mistakes more or less disastrous until he improves it.

Inaccuracy is one of the commonest failings, because accuracy is closely allied to self-discipline, and self-discipline, along with that glad subjection to external discipline which it involves, is an indication of high moral culture to which the majority have not yet attained. If the inaccurate man will not willingly subject himself to the discipline of his employer or instructor, but thinks he knows better, his failing can never be remedied, and he will thereby bind himself down to an inferior position, if in the business world; or to imperfect knowledge, if in the world of thought.

The prevalence of the vice of inaccuracy (and in view of its disastrous effect it must be regarded as a vice, though perhaps one of the lesser vices) is patent to every observe in the way in which the majority of people relate a circumstance or repeat a simple statement of fact. It is nearly always made untrue by more or less marked inaccuracies. Few people, perhaps (not reckoning those who deliberately lie), have trained themselves to be accurate in what they say, or are so careful as to admit and state their liability to error, and from this common form of inaccuracy many untruths and misunderstandings arise.

More people take pains to be accurate in what they do than in what they say, but even here inaccuracy is very common, rendering many inefficient and incompetent, and unfitting them for any strenuous and well sustained endeavour. The man who habitually uses up a portion of his own or his employer's time in trying to correct his errors, or for the correction of whose mistakes another has to be employed, is not the man to maintain any position in the work a day world; much less to reach a place among the ranks of the prosperous.

There never yet lived a man who did not make some mistakes on his way to his particular success, but he is the capable and right minded man who perceives his mistakes and quickly remedies them, and who is glad when they are pointed out to him. It is habitual and persistent; inaccuracy which is a vice; and he is the incapable and wrong minded man who will not see or admit his mistakes, and who takes offence when they are pointed out to him.

The progressive man learns by his own mistakes as well as by the mistakes of others. He is always ready to test good advice by practice, and aims at greater and ever greater accuracy in his methods, which means higher and higher perfection, for accuracy is perfect, and the measure of a man's accuracy will be the measure of his uniqueness and perfection.

Utility or usefulness, is the direct result of method in one's work. Labour arrives at fruitful and profitable ends when it is systematically pursued. If the gardener is to gather in the best produce, he must not only sow and plant, but he must sow and plant at the right time; and if any work is to be fruitful in results, it must be done seasonably, and the time for doing a thing must not be allowed to pass by.

Utility considers the practical end; and employs the best means to reach that end. It avoids side issues, dispenses with theories, and retains its hold only on those things which can appropriated to good uses in the economy of life.

Unpractical people burden their minds with useless and unverifiable theories, and court failure by entertaining speculations which, by their very nature, cannot be applied in practice. The man whose powers are shown in what he does, and not in mere talking are arguing, avoids metaphysical quibbling and quandaries, and applies himself to the accomplishment of some good and useful end.

That which cannot be reduced to practice should not be allowed to hamper the mind. It should be thrown aside, abandoned, and ignored. A man recently told me that if his theory should be proved to have no useful end, he should still retain his hold upon it as a beautiful theory. If a man chooses to cling to so-called "beautiful" theories which are proved to have no use in life, and no substantial basis of reality, he must not be surprised if he fails in his worldly undertakings, for he is an unpractical man.

When the powers of the mind are diverted from speculative theorizing to practical doing, whether in material or moral directions, skill, power, knowledge, and prosperity increase. A man's prosperity is measured by his usefulness to the community, and a man is useful in accordance with that he does, and not because of the theories which he entertains.

The carpenter fashions a chair; the builder erects a house; the mechanic produces a machine; and the wise man moulds a perfect character. Not the schismatic, the theorists and the controversialists, but the workers, the makers, and the doers are the salt of the earth.

Let a man turn away from the mirages of intellectual speculation, and begin to do something, and to do it with all his might, and he will thereby gain a special knowledge, wield a special power, and reach his own unique position and prosperity among his fellows.

Comprehensiveness is that quality of mind which enables a man to deal with a large number of related details, to grasp them in their entirety, along with the single principle which governs them and binds them together. It is a masterly quality, giving organizing and governing power, and is developed by systematic attention to details. The successful merchant holds in his mind, as it were, all the details of his business, and regulates them by a system adapted to his particular form of trade. The inventor has in his mind all the details of his machine, along with their relation to a central mechanical principle, and so perfects his invention. The author of a great poem or story relates all his characters and incidents to a central plot, and so produces a composite and enduring literary work. Comprehensiveness is analytic and synthetic capacity combined in the same individual. A capacious and well-ordered mind, which holds within its silent depths an army of details in their proper arrangement and true working order, is the mind that is near to genius, even if it has not already arrived. Every man cannot be a genius nor does he need to be, but he can be gradually evolving his mental capacity by careful attention to system in his thoughts and business, and as his intellect depends and broadens his powers will be intensified and his prosperity accentuated.

Such, then, are four corner pillars in the Temple of Prosperity, and of themselves they are sufficient to permanently sustain it without the addition of the remaining four. The man who perfects himself in Energy, Economy, Integrity, and System will achieve an enduring success in the work of his life, no matter what the nature of that work may be. It is impossible for one to fail who is full of energy, who carefully economizes his time and money, and virtuously husbands his vitality, who practices unswerving integrity, and who systematizes his work by first systematizing his mind.

Such a man's efforts will be rightly directed, and that, too, with concentrated power, so that they will be effective and fruitful. In addition he will reach a manliness and an independent dignity which will unconsciously command respect and success, and will strengthen weaker ones by its very presence in their midst. "Seest thou a man diligent in business; he shall stand before kings, he shall not stand before mean men," says Scripture of such a one. He will not beg, or whimper, or complain, or cynically blame others, but will be too strong and pure and upright a man to sink himself so low. And so standing high in the nobility and integrity of his character, he will fill a high place in the world and in the estimation of men. His success will be certain and his prosperity will endure. "He will stand and not fall in the battle of life."

6. Fifth pillar – Sympathy

The remaining pillars are the four central pillars in the Temple of Prosperity. They give it greater strength and stability, and add both to its beauty and utility. They contribute greatly to its attractiveness, for they belong to the highest moral sphere, and therefore to great beauty and nobility of character. They, indeed, make a man great, and place him among the comparatively few whose minds are rare, and that shine apart in sparkling purity and bright intelligence.

Sympathy should not be confounded with that maudlin and superficial sentiment which, like a pretty flower without root, presently perishes and leaves behind neither seed nor fruit. To fall into hysterical some suffering abroad, is not sympathy. Neither are bursts of violent indignation against the cruelties and injustices of others nor any indication of a sympathetic mind. If one is cruel at home – if he badgers his wife, or beats his children, or abuses his servants, or stabs his neighbors with shafts of bitter sarcasm what hypocrisy is in his profession of love for suffering people who are outside the immediate range of his influence! What shallow sentiment informs his bursts of indignation against the injustice and hard heartedness in the world around him.

Says Emerson of such – "Go, love thy infant; love thy wood chopper; be good natured and modest; have that grace; and never varnish your hard uncharitable ambition with this incredible tenderness for black folk a thousand miles off. Thy love afar is spite at home." The test of a man is in his immediate acts, and not in ultra sentiments; and if those acts are consistently informed with selfishness and bitterness, if those at home hear his steps with dread, and feel a joyful relief on his departure, how empty are his expressions of sympathy for the suffering or down trodden how futile his membership of a philanthropic society.

Though the well of sympathy may feed the spring of tears, that spring more often draws its supply from the dark pool of selfishness, for when selfishness is thwarted it spends itself in tears.

Sympathy is a deep, silent, inexpressible tenderness which is shown in a consistently self-forgetful gentle character. Sympathetic people are not gushing and spasmodic, but are permanently self-restrained, firm, quiet, unassuming and gracious. Their undisturbed demeanour, where the suffering of others is concerned, is frequently mistaken for indifference by shallow minds, but the sympathetic and discerning eye recognizes, in their quiet strength and their swiftness to aid while others are sweeping, and wronging their hands, the deepest, soundest sympathy.

Lack of sympathy is shown in cynicism, ill-natured sarcasm, bitter ridicule, taunting and mockery, and anger and condemnation, as well as in that morbid and false sentiment which is a theoretical and assumed sympathy, having no basis in practice.

Lack of sympathy arises in egotism; sympathy arises in love. Egotism is involved in ignorance; love is allied to knowledge. It is common with men to imagine themselves as separate from their fellows, with separate aims and interests; and to regard themselves as right and others wrong in their respective ways. Sympathy lifts a man above this separate and self-centred life and enables him to live in the hearts of his fellows, and to think and feel with them. He puts himself in their place, and becomes, for the time being, as they are. As Whitman, the hospital hero, expresses it – "I do not ask the wounded person." It is a kind of impertinence to question a suffering creature. Suffering calls for aid and tenderness, and not for curiosity; and the sympathetic man or woman feels the suffering, and ministers to its alleviation.

Nor can sympathy boast, and wherever self-praise enters in, sympathy passes out. If one speaks of his many deeds of kindness, and complains of the ill treatment he has received in return, he has not done kindly deeds, but has yet to reach that self-forgetful modest which is the sweetness of sympathy.

Sympathy, in its real and profound sense, is oneness with others in their strivings and sufferings, so that the man of sympathy is a composite being; he is, as it were, a number of men, and he views a thing from a number of different sides, and not from one side only, and that his own particular side. He sees with the others men's eyes, hears with their ears, thinks with their minds, and feels with their hearts. He is thus able to understand men who are vastly different from himself; the meaning of their lives is revealed to him, and he is united to them in the spirit of goodwill. Said Balzac – "The poor fascinate me; their hunger is my hunger; I am with them in their homes; their privations I suffer; I feel the beggar's rags upon my back; I for the time being become the poor and despised man." It reminds us of the saying of One greater than Balzac, that a deed done for a suffering little one was done for him.

And so it is; sympathy leads us to the hearts of all men, so that we become spiritually united to them, and when they suffer we feel the pain; when they are glad we rejoice with them; when they are despised and persecuted, we spiritually descend with them into the depths, and take into our hearts their humiliation and distress; and he who has this binding, uniting spirit of sympathy, can never be cynical and condemnatory, can never pass thoughtless and cruel judgements upon his fellows; because in his tenderness of heart he is ever with them in their pain.

But to have reached this ripened sympathy, it must needs be that one has loved much, suffered much and sounded the dark depths of sorrow. It springs from acquaintance with the profoundest experiences, so that a man has ad conceit, thoughtlessness, and selfishness burnt out of his heart. No man can have true sympathy who has not been, in some measure at least, "a man of sorrows, and acquainted with grief," but the sorrow and grief must have passed, must have ripened into a fixed kindness and habitual calm.

To have suffered so much in a certain direction that the suffering is finished, and only its particular wisdom remains, enables one, wherever that suffering presents itself, to understand and deal with it by pure sympathy; and when one has been "perfected by suffering" in many directions, he becomes a centre of rest and healing for the sorrowing and broken hearted who are afflicted with the affections which he has experienced and conquered. As a mother feels the anguish of her suffering child, so the man of sympathy feels the anguish of suffering men.

Such is the highest and holiest sympathy, but a sympathy much less perfect is a great power for good in human life and a measure of it is everywhere and every day needed. While rejoicing in the fact that in every walk in life there are truly sympathetic people, one also perceives that harshness, resentment, and cruelty are all too common. These hard qualities bring their own sufferings, and there are those who fail in their business, or particular work, entirely because of the harshness of their disposition. A man who is fiery and resentful, or who is hard, cold and calculating, with the springs of sympathy dried up within him, even though he be otherwise an able man, will, in the end scarcely avoid disaster in his affairs. His heated folly in the one case, or cold cruelty in the other, will gradually isolate him from his fellows and from those who are immediately related to him in his particular avocation, so that the elements of prosperity will be eliminated from his life, leaving him with a lonely failure, and perhaps a hopeless despair.

Even in ordinary business transactions, sympathy is an important factor, for people will always be attracted to those who are of a kindly and genial nature, preferring to deal with them rather than with those who are hard and forbidding. In all spheres where direct personal contact plays an important part, the sympathetic man with average ability will always take precedence of the man of greater ability but who is unsympathetic.

If a man be a minister or a clergyman, a cruel laugh or an unkind sentence from him will seriously injure his reputation and influence, but particularly his influence, for even they who admire his good qualities will, through his unkindness, unconsciously have a lower regard for him in their personal esteem.

If a business man profess religion, people will expect to see the good influence of that religion on his business transactions. To profess to be a worshipper of the gentle Jesus on Sunday, and all the rest of the wee be a hard, grasping worshipper of mammon, will injure his trade, and detract considerably from his prosperity.

Sympathy is a universal spiritual language which all, even the animals, instinctively understand and appreciate, for all beings and creatures are subject to suffering, and this sameness of painful experience leads to that unity of feeling which we call sympathy.

Selfishness impels men to protect themselves at the expense of others; but sympathy impels them to protect others by the sacrifice of self; and in this sacrifice of self there is no real and ultimate loss, for while the pleasure of selfishness are small and few, the blessings of sympathy are great and manifold.

It may be asked, "How can a businessman; whose object is to develop his own trade, practice self-sacrifice?" Even man can practice self-sacrifice just where he is, and in the measure that he is capable of understand it. If one contends that he cannot practice a virtue it, for were his circumstances different, he would still have the same excuse. Diligence in business is not incompatible with self-sacrifice, for devotion to duty, even though that duty be trade, is not selfishness, but may be an unselfish devotion. I know a businessman who, when a competitor who had tried to 'cut him out' in business, cut himself out and failed, set that same competitor up in business again. Truly a beautiful act of self-sacrifice; and the man that did it is, today, one of the most successful and prosperous of businessmen.

The most prosperous commercial traveler I have ever known, was overflowing with exuberant kindness and geniality. He was as innocent of all "tricks of trade" as a new born infant, but his great heart and manly uprightness won for him fast friends wherever he went. Men were glad to see him come into their office or shop or mill, and not alone for the good and bracing influence he brought with him, but also because his business was sound and trustworthy. This man was successful through sheer sympathy, but sympathy so pure and free from policy, that he himself would probably have denied that his success could be attributed to it. Sympathy can never hinder success. It is selfishness that blights and destroys. As goodwill increases, man's prosperity will increase. All interests are mutual, and stand or fall together, and as sympathy expands the heart, it extends the circle of influence, making blessings, both spiritual and material, to more greatly abound.

Fourfold are the qualities which make up the great virtue of sympathy, namely:-

1. Kindness
2. Generosity
3. Gentleness
4. Insight

Kindness, when fully developed, is not a passing impulse but a permanent quality. An intermittent and unreliable impulse is not kindness, though it often goes under that name. There is no kindness in praise if it be followed by abuse. The love which seems to prompt the spontaneous kiss will be of little account if it be associated with a spontaneous spite. The gift which seemed so gracious will lose its value should the giver afterwards wish its value in return. To have one's feelings aroused to do a kind action towards another by some external stimulus pleasing to one's self, and shortly afterwards to be swayed to the other extreme towards the same person by an external event unpleasing to one's self, should be regarded as weakness of character; and it is also a selfish condition, us, and when he pleases us, to be thinking of one's self only. A true kindness is unchangeable, and needs no external stimulus to force it into action. It is a well from which thirsty souls can always drink, and it never runs dry. Kindness, when it is a strong virtue, is bestowed not only on those who please us, but also upon those whose actions go contrary to our wish and will, and it is a constant and never – varying glow of genial warmth.

There are some actions of which men repent; such are all unkind actions. There are other actions of which men do not repent, and such are all kind actions. The day comes when men are sorry for the cruel things they said and did; but the day of gladness is always with them for the kindly things they have said and done.

Unkindness mars a man's character, it mars his face as time goes on, and it mars that perfection of success which he would otherwise reach.

Kindness beautifies the character, it beautifies the face with the growth of the years, and it enables a man to reach that perfection of success to which his intellectual abilities entitle him. A man's prosperity is mellowed and enriched by the kindness of his disposition.

Generosity goes with a larger hearted kindness. If kindness be the gentle sister, Generosity is the strong brother. A free, open handed, and magnanimous character is always attractive and influential. Stringiness and meanness always repel; they are dark, cramped, narrow, and cold. Kindness and generosity always attack; they are sunny, genial, open, and warm. That which repels makes for isolation and failure; that which attracts makes for union and success.

Giving is as important a duty as getting; and he who gets all he can, and refuses to give, will at last be unable to get; for it is as much a spiritual law that we cannot get unless we give, as that we cannot give unless we get.

Giving has always been taught as a great and important duty by all the religious teachers. This is because giving is one of the highways of personal growth and progress. It is a means by which we attain to greater and greater unselfishness, and by which we prevent the falling back into selfishness. It implies that we recognize our spiritual and social kinship with our fellowmen, and are willing to part with a portion of that we have earned or possess, for man who, the more he gets, hungers for more still, and refuses to loosen his grasp upon his accumulating store, like a wild beast with its prey, is retrogressing; he is shutting himself out from all the higher and joy giving qualities, and from free and life giving communion with unselfish, happy human hearts. Dickens's Scrooge in "A Christmas Carol" represents the condition of such a man with graphic vividness and dramatic force.

Our public men in England today (probably also in America) are nearly all (I think I might say all, for I have not yet met an exception) great givers. These men – Lord Mayors, Mayors, Magistrates, Town and City Councillors, and all men filling responsible public offices – being men who have been singularly successful in the management of their own private affairs, are considered the best men for the management of public affairs, and numerous noble institutions throughout the land are perpetual witnesses to the munificence of their gifts. Nor have I been able to find any substantial truth in the accusation, so often hurled against such men by the envious and unsuccessful, that their riches are made unjustly. Without being perfect men, they are an honourable class of manly, vigorous, generous, and successful men, who have acquired riches and honour by sheer industry, ability and uprightness.

Let a man beware of greed, of meanness, of envy, of jealousy, of suspicion, for these things, if harboured, will rob him of all that is best in life, aye, even all that is best in material things, as well as all that is best in character and happiness. Let him be liberal of heart and generous of hand, magnanimous and trusting, not only giving cheerfully and often of his substance, but allowing his friends and fellow men freedom of thought and action – let him be thus, and honour, plenty, and prosperity will come knocking at the door for admittance as his friends and guests.

Gentleness is akin to divinity. Perhaps no quality is so far removed from all that is coarse, brutal and selfish as gentleness, so that when one is becoming gentle, he is becoming divine. It can only be acquired after much experience and through great self-discipline. It only becomes established in a man's heart when he has controlled and brought into subjection his animal voice, a distinct, firm, but quiet enunciation, and freedom from excitement, vehemence, or resentment in peculiarly aggravating circumstances.

If there is one quality which, above all others, should distinguish the religious man, it is the quality of gentleness, for it is the hall mark of spiritual culture. The rudely aggressive man is an affront to cultivated minds and unselfish hearts. Our word gentlemen has not altogether departed from its original meaning. It is still applied to one who is modest and self-restrained, and is considerate for the feelings and welfare of others. A gentle man one whose good behavior is prompted by thoughtfulness and kindliness is always loved, whatever may be his origin. Quarrelsome people make a display in their bickering and recriminations – of their ignorance and lack of culture. The man who has perfected himself in gentleness never quarrels. He never returns the hard word; he leaves it alone, or meets it with a gentle word which is far more powerful than wrath. Gentleness is wedded to wisdom, and the wise man has overcome all anger in himself, and so understands how to overcome it in others. The gentleman is saved from most of the disturbances and turmoils with which uncontrolled men afflict themselves. While they are wearing themselves out with wasteful and needless strain, he is quiet and composed, and such quietness and composure are strong to win in the battle of life.

Insight is the gift of sympathy. The sympathetic mind is the profoundly perceiving mind. We understand by experience, and not by argument. Before we can know a thing or being, our life must touch its or his life. Argument analyzes the outer skin, but sympathy reaches to the heart. The cynic sees the hat and coat, and thinks he sees the man. The sympathetic seer sees the man, and is not concerned with the hat and coat. In all kinds of hatred there is a separation by which each misjudges the other. In all kinds of love there is a mystic union by which each knows the other. Sympathy, being the purest form of this the greatest poet because he has the largest heart. No other figure in all literature has shown such a profound knowledge of the human heart, and of nature both animate and inanimate. The personal Shakespeare is not to be found in his works; he is merged, by sympathy, into his characters. The wise man and the philosopher; the madman and the fool; the drunkard and the harlot – these he, for the time fit into their particular experiences and knew them better than they knew themselves. Shakespeare has no partiality, no prejudice; his sympathy embraces all, from the lowest to the highest.

Prejudice is the great barrier to sympathy and knowledge. It is impossible to understand those against whom one harbours a prejudice. We only see men and things as they are when we divest our minds of partial judgements. We become seers as we become sympathizers. Sympathy has knowledge for her companion.

Inseparable are the feeling heart and the seeing eye. The man of pity is the man of prophecy. He whose heart beats in tune with all hearts, to him the contents of all hearts are revealed. Nor are past and future any longer insoluble mysteries to the man of sympathy. His moral insight apprehends the perfect round of human life.

Sympathetic insight lifts a man into the consciousness of freedom, gladness and power. His spirit inhales joy as his lungs inhale air. There are no longer any fears of his fellow-men of competition, hard times, enemies, and the like. These grovelling illusion have disappeared, and there has opened up before his awakened vision a realm of greatness and grandeur.

7. Sixth pillar – Sincerity

Human society is held together by its sincerity. A universal falseness would beget a universal mistrust which would bring about a universal separation, if not destruction. Life is made sane, wholesome, and happy, by our deep rooted belief in one another. If we did not trust men, we could not transact business with them, could not even associate with them. Shakespeare's "Timon" shows us the wretched condition of a man who, through his own folly, has lost all faith in the sincerity of human nature. He cuts himself off from the company of all men, and finally commits suicide. Emerson has something to the effect that if the trust system were withdrawn from commerce, society would fall to pieces; that system being an indication of the universal confidence men place in each other. Business, commonly supposed by the shortsighted and foolish to be all fraud and deception is based on a great trust – a trust that men will meet and fulfil their obligations. Payment is not asked until the goods are delivered; and the fact of the continuance of this system for ages, proves that most men do pay their debts, and have no wish to avoid such payment.

Back of all its shortcomings, human society rests on a strong basis of truth. Its fundamental note in sincerity. Its great leaders are all men of superlative sincerity; and their names and achievements are not allowed to perish – a proof that the virtue of sincerity is admired by all the race.

It is easy for the insincere to imagine that everybody is like themselves, and to speak of the "rottenness of society," - though a rotten thing could endure age after age, for is not everything yellow to the jaundiced eye? People who cannot see anything good in the constitution of human society, should overhaul themselves. Their trouble is near home. They call good, evil. They have dwelt cynically and peevishly on evil till they cannot see good, and everything and everybody appears evil. "Society is rotten from top to bottom," I heard a man say recently; and he asked me if I did not think so. I replied that I should be sorry to think so; that while society had many blemishes, it was sound at the core, and contained within itself the seeds of perfection.

Society, indeed is so sound that the man who is playing a part for the accomplishment of entirely selfish ends cannot long prosper, and cannot fill any place as an influence. He is soon unmasked and disagreed; and the fact that such a man can, for even a brief period, batten on human credulity, speaks well for the trustfulness of men, if it reveals their lack of wisdom.

An accomplished actor on the stage is admired, but the designing actor on the stage of life brings himself down to ignominy and contempt. In striving to appear what he is not, he becomes as one having no individuality, no character, and he is deprived of all influence, all power, all success.

A man of profound sincerity is a great moral force, and there is no force – not even the highest intellectual force – that can compare with it. Men are powerful in influence according to the soundness and perfection of their sincerity. Morality and sincerity are so closely bound up together, that where sincerity is lacking, morality, as a power, is lacking also, for insincerity undermines all the other virtues, so that they crumble away and become of no account. Even a little insincerity robs a character of all its nobility, and makes it common and contemptible. Falseness is so despicable a vice and no man of moral weight can afford to dally with pretty complements, or play the fool with trivial and howsoever light, in order to please, and he is no longer strong and admirable, but is become a shallow weakling whose mind has no deep well of power from which men can draw, and no satisfying richness to stir in them a worshipful regard.

Even they who are for the moment flattered with the painted lie, or pleased with the deftly woven deception, will not escape those permanent under currents of influence which move the heart and shape the judgement to fixed and final issues, while these designed delusions create but momentary ripples on the surface of the mind.

"I am very pleased with his attentions," said a woman of an acquaintance, "but I would not marry him." "Why not?" she was asked. "He doesn't ring true," was the reply.

Ring true, a term full of meaning. It has reference to the coin which, when tested by its ring, emits a sound which reveals the sterling metal throughout, without the admixture of any base material. It comes up to the standard, and will pass anywhere and everywhere for its full value.

So with men. Their words and actions emit their own peculiar influence. There is in them an inaudible sound which all other men inwardly hear and instinctively detect. They know the false ring from the true, yet know not how they know. As the outer ear can make the most delicate distinctions in sounds, so the inner ear can make equally subtle distinctions between souls. None are ultimately deceived but the deceiver. It is the blind folly of the insincere that, while flattering themselves upon their successful simulations, they are deceiving none but themselves. Their actions are laid bare before all hearts. There is at the heart of man a tribunal whose judgements do not miscarry. If the senses faultlessly detect, shall not the soul infallibly know! This inner infallibility is shown in the collective judgement of the race. This judgement is perfect; so perfect that in literature, art, science, invention, religion – in every department of knowledge – it divides the good from the bad, the worthy from the unworthy, the true from the false, zealously guarding and preserving the former, and allowing the latter to perish. The works, words, and deeds of great men are the heirlooms of the race, and the race is not careless of their value. A thousand men write a book, and one only is a work of original genius, yet the race singles out that one, elevates and preserves it, while it consigns the nine hundred and ninety nine copyists to oblivion. Ten thousand men utter a sentence under a similar circumstance, and one only is a sentence of divine wisdom, yet the race singles out that saying for the guidance of posterity, while the other sentences are heard no more. It is true that the race slays its prophets, but even that slaying becomes a test which reveals the true ring, and men detect its tureens. The slain one has come up to the standard, and the deed of his slaying is preserved as furnishing infallible proof of his greatness.

As the counterfeit coin is detected, and cast back into the melting pot, while the sterling coin circulates among all men, and is valued for its worth, so the counterfeit word, deed, or character is perceived, and is left to fall back into the nothingness from which it emerged, a thing unreal, powerless, dead.

Spurious things have no value, whether they be bric-a-brac or men. We are ashamed of imitations that try to pass for the genuine article. Falseness is cheap. The masquerader becomes a byword; he is less than a man; he is a shadow, a spook, a mere mask. Trueness is valuable. The sound hearted man becomes an exemplar; he is more than a man; he is a reality; a force, a moulding principle, by falseness all is lost – even individuality dissolves for falseness is nonentity, nothingness. By trueness everything is gained, for trueness is fixed, permanent, real.

It is all important that we be real; that we harbour no wish to appear other than what we are; that we simulate no virtue, assume no excellency, adopt no disguise. The hypocrite thinks he can hood wink the world and the eternal law of the world. There is but one person that he hoodwinks, and that is himself, and for that the law of the world inflicts its righteous penalty. There is an old theory that the excessively wicked are annihilated. I think to be a pretender is to come as near to annihilation as a man can get, for there is a sense in which the man is gone, and in his place there is but a mirage of shams. The hell of annihilation which so many dread, he has descended into; and to think that such a man can prosper is to think that shadows can do the work of entities, and displace real men.

If any man thinks he can build up a successful career on pretences and appearances, let him pause before sinking into the abyss of shadows; for in insincerity there is no solid ground, no substance, no reality; there is nothing on which anything can stand, and no material with which to build; but there are loneliness, poverty, shame, confusion, fears, suspicions, weeping, groaning, and lamentations; for if there is one hell lower, darker, fouler than all others, it is the hell of insincerity.

Four beautiful traits adorn the mind of the sincere man; they are:-

1. Simplicity
2. Attractiveness
3. Penetration
4. Power

Simplicity is naturalness. It is simple being, without fake or foreign adornment. Why are all things in nature so beautiful? Because they are natural. We see them as they are, no task they might wish to appear, for in sooth they have no wish to appear, for in sooth they have no wish to appear otherwise. There is no hypocrisy in the world of nature outside of human nature. The flower which is so beautiful in all eyes would lose its beautify in all eyes would nature we look upon reality, and its beauty and perfection gladden and amaze us. We cannot find anywhere a flaw, and are conscious of our incapacity to improve upon anything, even to the most insignificant. Everything has its own peculiar perfection, and shines in the beauty of unconscious simplicity.

One of the modern social cries is, "Back to nature." It is generally understood to mean a cottage in the country, and a piece of land to cultivate. It will be of little use to go into the country if we take our shams with us; and any veneer which may cling to us can as well be washed off just where we are. It is good that they who feel burdened with the conventions of society should fly to the country, and court the quiet of nature, but it will fail if it by anything but a means to that inward redemption which will restore us to the simple and the true.

But though humanity has wandered from the natural simplicity of the animal world, it is moving towards a higher, a divine simplicity. Men of great genius are such because of their spontaneous simplicity. They do not foreign; they are. Lesser minds study style and effect. They wish to cut a striking figure on the stage of the world, and by that unholy wish they are doomed to mediocrity. Said a man to me recently, "I would give twenty years of my life to be able to write an immortal hymn." With such an ambition a man cannot write a hymn. He wants to pose. He is thinking of himself, of his own glory. Before a man can writer an immortal hymn, or create any immortal work he must give, not twenty years of his life to ambition but his can do anything great, and must sing, paint, write, out of ten thousand bitter experiences, ten thousand failures, ten thousand conquests, ten thousand joys. He must know Gethsemane; he must work with blood and tears.

Retaining his intellect and moral powers, and returning to simplicity, a man becomes great. He forfeits nothing real. Only the shams are cast aside, revealing the standard gold of character. Where there is sincerity there will always be simplicity – a simplicity of the kind that we see in nature, the beautiful simplicity of truth.

Attractiveness is the direct outcome of simplicity. This is seen in the attractiveness of all natural objects; to which we have referred, but in human nature it is manifested as personal influence. Of recent years certain pseudomystics have been advertising to sell the secret of "personal magnetism" for so many dollars, by which they purport to show vain people how they can make themselves attractive to others by certain "occult" means as though attractiveness can be bought and sold, and put on and off like powder and paint. Nor are people who are anxious to be thought attractive, likely to become so, for their vanity is a barrier to it. The very desire to be thought attractive is, in itself, a deception, and it leads to the practice of numerous deceptions. It infers, too, that such people are conscious of lacking the genuine attractions and graces of character, and are on the lookout for a substitute; but there is no substitute for beauty of mind and strength of character. Attractiveness, like genius, is lost by being coveted, and possessed by those who are too solid and sincere of character to desire it. There is nothing in human nature – nor talent, nor intellect, nor affection, nor beauty of features that can compare in attractive power with that soundness of mind and wholeness of heart which we call sincerity. There is a perennial charm about a sincere man or woman, and they draw about themselves the best specimens of human nature. There can be no personal charm apart from sincerity. Infatuation there may be, and is, but this is a kind of disease, and is vastly different from the indissoluble bond by which sincere people are attached. Infatuation ends in painful disillusion, but as there is nothing hidden between sincere souls, and they stand upon that solid ground of reality, there is no illusion to be displayed.

Leaders among men attract by the power of their sincerity, and the measures of their sincerity is the measure of their sincerity is the great may be a man's intellect he can never be a permanent leader and guide of men unless he be sincere. For a time he may sail jauntily upon the stream of popularity, and believe himself secure, but it is only that he may shortly fall the lower in popular odium. He cannot long deceive the people with his painted front. They will soon look behind, and find of what spurious stuff he is made. He is like a woman with a painted face. She thinks she is admired for her complexion, but all know it is paint, and despise her for it. she has one admirer – herself, and the hell of limitation to which all the insincere commit themselves is the hell of self-admiration.

Sincere people do not think of themselves, of their talent, their genius, their virtue, their beautify and because they are so unconscious of themselves, they attract all, and win their confidence, affection, and esteem.

Penetration belongs to the sincere. All shams are unveiled in their presence. All simulators are transparent to the searching eye of the sincere man. With one clear glance he sees through all their flimsy pretences. Tricksters with under his strong gaze, and want to get away from it. He who has rid his heart of all falseness, and entertains only that which is true, has gained the power to distinguish the false from the true in others. He is not deceived who is not self-deceived.

As men, looking around on the objects of nature, infallibly distinguish them such as a snake, a bird, a horse, a tree, a rose, and so on – so the sincere man distinguishes between the variety of characters. He perceives in a movement, a look, a word, an act, the nature of the man, and acts accordingly. He is on his guard without being suspicious. He is prepared for the pretender without being mistrustful. He acts from positive knowledge, and not from negative suspicion. Men are open to him, and he reads their contents. His penetrative judgement pierces to the centre of actions. His direct and unequivocal conduct strengthens in others the good, and shames the bad, and he is a staff of strength to those who have not yet attained to his soundness of heart and head.

Power goes with penetration. An understanding of the nature of actions is accompanied with the power to meet and deal with all actions in the right and best way. Knowledge is always power, but knowledge of the nature of actions is superlative power, and he who possesses it becomes a Presence to all hearts, and modifies their actions for good. Long after his bodily presence has passed away, he is still a moulding force in the world and is a spiritual reality working subtly in the minds of men, and shaping them towards sublime ends. At first his power local and limited, but the circle of righteousness which he has set moving, continues to extend and extended till it embraces the whole world, and all men are influenced by it.

The sincere man stamps his character upon all that he does, and also upon all people with whom he comes in contact. He speaks a word in season, and some one is impressed; the influence is communicated to another, and another, and presently some despairing soul ten thousand miles away hears it and is restored. Such a power is prosperity in itself, and its worth is not to be valued in coin. Money cannot purchase the priceless jewels of character, but labour in right doing can, and he who makes himself sincere, who acquires a robust soundness throughout his entire being, will become a man of singular success and rare power.

Such is the strong pillar of sincerity. It supporting power is to great that, one it is completely erected, the Temple of Prosperity is secure. Its walls will not crumble; its rafters will not decay; its roof will not fall in. It will stand while the man lives, and when has passed away it will continue to afford a shelter and a home for others through many generation.

8. Seventh pillar – Impartiality

To get rid of prejudice is a great achievement. Prejudices piles obstacles in a man's way – obstacles to health, success, happiness, and prosperity, so that he is continually running up against imaginary enemies, who, when prejudice is removed, are seen to be friend. Life, indeed, a sort of obstacle race to the man of prejudice, a race wherein the obstacles cannot be negotiated and the goal is not reached; whereas to the impartial man life is a day's walk in a pleasant country, with refreshment and rest at the end of the day.

To acquire impartiality, a man must remove that innate egotism which prevents him from seeing any thing from any point of view other than this own. A great task, truly; but a notable, and one that can be well begun now, even if it cannot be finished. Truth can "remove mountains", and prejudice is a range of mental mountains beyond which the partisan does not see, and of which he does not believe there is any beyond. These mountains removed, however, there opens to the view the unending vista of mental variety blended in one glorious picture of light and shade, of colour and tone, gladdening beholding eyes.

By clinging to stubborn prejudice what joys are missed, what friends are sacrificed, what happiness is destroyed, and what prospects are blighted! And yet freedom from prejudice is a rare thing. There are few men who are not prejudiced partisans upon the subjects which are of interest to them. One rarely meets a man that will dispassionately discuss his subject from both sides, considering all the facts and weighing all the evidence so as to arrive at truth on the matter. Each partisan has his own case to make out. He is not searching for truth, for he is already convinced that his own conclusion is the truth, and that all else is error; but he is defending his own case, and striving for victory. Neither does he attempt to prove that he has the truth by a calm array of facts and evidence, but defends his position with more or less heat and agitation.

Prejudice causes a man to form a conclusion, sometimes without any basis of fact or knowledge, and then to refuse to consider anything which does not support that conclusion; and in this way prejudice is a complete barrier to the attainment of knowledge. It binds a man down to darkness and ignorance, and prevents the development of his mind in the highest and noblest directions. More than this, it also shuts him out from communion with the best minds, and confines him to the dark and solitary cell of his own egotism.

Prejudice is a shutting up of the mind against the entrance of new light, against the perception of more beauty, against the hearing of diviner music. The partisan clings to his little, fleeting, flimsy opinion, and thinks it the greatest thing in the world. He is so in love with his own conclusion (which is only a form of self-love), that he thinks all men ought to agree with him, and he regards men as more or less stupid who do not see as he sees, while he praises the good judgement of those who are one with him in his view. Such a man cannot have knowledge, cannot have truth. He is confined to the sphere of opinion (to his own self-created illusions) which is outside the realm of reality. He moves in a kind of self-infatuation which prevents him from seeing the commonest facts of life, while his own theories – usually more or less groundless – assume, in his mind, overpowering proportions. He fondly imagines that there is but one side to everything, and that side is his own. There are at least two sides to everything, and he it is who finds the truth in a matter who carefully examines both sides with all freedom from excitement, and without any desire for the predominance of one side over another.

In its divisions and controversies the world at large is like two lawyers defending a case. The counsel for the prosecution presents all the facts which prove his side, while counsel for the defense presents all the facts which support his contention, and each belittles or ignores, or tries to reason away, the facts of the other. The Judge in the case, however, is like the impartial thinker among men: having listened to all the evidence on both sides, he compares and sifts it so as to form an impartial summing up in the cause of justice.

Not that this universal partiality is a bad thing, nor as in all other extremes, nature here reduces the oppositions of conflicting parties to a perfect balance; moreover, it is a factor in evolution; it stimulates men to think who have not yet developed the power to rouse up vigorous thought at will, and it is a phase through which all men have to pass. But it is only byway – and a tangled, confused and painful one – towards the great highway of Truth. It is the arc of which impartiality is the perfect round. The partisan sees a portion of the truth, and thinks it the whole, but the impartial thinker sees the whole truth which includes all sides. It is necessary that we find see truth in sections, as it were, until, having gathered up all the parts, we may piece them together and form the perfect circle, and the forming of such circle is the attainment of impartiality.

The impartial man examines, weighs, and considers, with freedom from prejudice and from likes and dislikes. His one wish is to discover the truth. He abolishes preconceived opinions, and lets facts and evidence speak for themselves. He has no case to make out for himself, for he knows that truth is unalterable, that his opinions can make no difference to it, and that it can be investigated and discovered. He thereby escapes a vast amount of friction and nervous wear and tear to which the feverish partisan is subject; and in addition, he looks directly upon the face of Reality, and so becomes tranquil and peaceful.

So rare is freedom from prejudice that wherever the impartial thinker may be, he is sure, sooner or later, to occupy a very high position in the estimation of the world, and in the guidance of its destiny. Not necessarily an office in worldly affairs, for that is improbable, but an exalted position in the sphere of influence. There may be such a one now, and he may be a carpenter, a weaver, a clerk; he may be in poverty or in the home of a millionaire; he may be short or tall, or of any complexion, but whatever and wherever he may be, he has, though unknown, already begun to move the world, and will one day be universally recognized at a new force and creative centre in evolution.

There was one such some nineteen hundred years ago. He was only a poor, unlettered carpenter; He was regarded as a madman by His own relatives, and he came to an ignominious end in the eyes of His countrymen, but He sowed the seeds of an influence which has altered the whole world.

There was another such in India some twenty five centuries ago. He was accomplished, highly educated, and was the son of a capitalist and landed proprietor a petty king. He became a penniless, homeless mendicant, and to day one third of the human race worship at his shrine, and are restrained and elevated by his influence.

"Beware when the great God lets loose a thinker on this plane," says Emerson; and a man is not a thinker who is bound by prejudice; he is merely the strenuous upholder of an opinion. Every idea must pass through the medium of his particular prejudice, and receive its colour, so that dispassionate thinking and impartial judgement are rendered impossible. Such a man sees everything only in its relation, or imagined relation, to his opinion, whereas the thinker sees things as they are. The man who has so purified his mind of prejudice and of all the imperfections of egotism as to be able to look directly upon reality, has reached the acme of power; he holds in his hands, as it were, the vastest influence, and he will wield this power whether he knows it or not; it will be inseparable from his life, and will go from him as perfume from the flower. It will be in his words, his deeds, in his bodily postures and the motions of his mind, even in his silence and the stillness of his frame. Wherever he goes, even though he should fly to the desert, he will not escape this lofty destiny, for a great thinker is the centre of the world; by him all men are held in their orbits and all thought gravitates towards him.

The true thinker lives above and beyond the seething whirlpool of passion in which mankind is engulfed. He is not swayed by personal consideration, for he has grasped the import of impersonal principles, and being thus a noncombatant in the clashing warfare of egotistic desires, he can, from the vantage ground of an impartial but not indifferent watcher, see both sides equally, and grasp the cause and meaning of the fray.

Not only the Great Teachers, but the greatest figures in literature, are those who are free from prejudice, who, like true mirrors, effect things impartially. Such are Whitman, Shakespeare, Balzac, Emerson, Homer. These minds are not local, but universal. Their attitude is cosmic and not personal.

They contain within themselves all things and beings all worlds and laws. They are the gods who guide the race, and who will bring it at last out of its fever of passion into their own serene land.

The true thinker is the greatest of men, and his destiny is the most exalted. The altogether impartial mind has reached the divine, and it basks in the full daylight of Reality.

The four great elements of impartiality are
1. Justice
2. Patience
3. Calmness

4. Wisdom

Justice is the giving and receiving of equal values. What is called "striking a hard bargain" is a kind of theft. It means that the purchaser gives value for only a portion of his purchase, the remainder being appropriated as clear gain. The seller also encourages it by closing the bargain.

The just man does not try to gain an advantage; he considers the true values of things, and moulds his transactions in accordance therewith. He does not let "what will pay" come before "what is right," for he knows that the right pays best in the end. He does not seek his own benefit to the disadvantage of another, for he knows that a just action benefits, equally and fully, both parties to a transaction. If "one man's loss is another man's gain," it is only that the balance may be adjusted later on. Unjust gains cannot lead to prosperity, but are sure to bring failure. A just man could no more take from another an unjust gain by what is called a "smart transaction" that he could take it by picking his pocket. He would regard the one as dishonest as the other.

The bargaining spirit in business is not the true spirit of commerce. It is the selfish and thieving spirit which wants to get something for nothing. The upright man purges his business of all bargaining, and builds it one the more dignified basis of justice. He supplies "a good article" at its right price, and does not alter. He does not soil his hands with any business which is tainted with fraud. His goods are genuine and they are properly priced.

Customers who try to "beat down" a tradesman in their purchases are degrading themselves. Their practice assumes one or both of two things, namely, that either the tradesman is dishonest and is overcharging (a low, suspicious attitude of mind), or that they are eager to cajole him out of his profit (an equally base attitude), and so benefit by his loss. The practice of "bearing down" is altogether a dishonest one, and the people who pursue it most assiduously are those who complain most of being "imposed on" and this is not surprising, seeing that they themselves are all the time trying to impose upon others.

On the other hand, the tradesman who is anxious to get all he can out of his customers, irrespective of justice and the right values of things, is a kind of robber, and is slowly poisoning his success, for his deeds will assuredly come home to him in the form of financial ruin.

Said a man of fifty to me other day, "I have just discovered that all my life I have been paying fifty percent, more for everything than I ought to." A just man cannot feel that he has ever paid too much for anything, for he does not close with any transaction which he considers unjust; but if a man is eager to get everything at half price, them he will be always meanly and miserably mourning that he is paying double for everything. The just man is glad to pay full value for everything, whether in giving or receiving and his mind is untroubled and his days are full of peace.

Let a man above all avoid meanness, and strive to be ever more and more perfectly just, for if not just, he can be neither honest, nor generous, nor manly, but is a kind of disguised thief trying to get all he can, and give back as little as possible. Let him eschew all bargaining, and teach bargainers a better way by conducting his business with that exalted dignity which commands a large and meritorious success.

Patience is the brightest jewel in the character of the impartial man. Not a particular patience with a particular thing – like a girl with her needlework, or a boy building his toy engine but on unswerving considerateness, a sweetness of disposition at all times and under the most trying circumstances, an unchangeable and gentle strength which no trial can mar and no persecution can break. A rare possession, it is true, and one not to be expected for a long time yet from the bulk of mankind, but a virtue that can be reached by degree, and even a partial patience will work wonders in a man's life and affairs, as a confirmed impatience all work devastation. The irascible man is courting speedy disaster, for who will care to deal with a man who continually going off like ground powder when some small spark of complaint or criticism falls upon him! Even his friends will one by one desert him, for who would court the company of a man who rudely assaults him with an impatient and fiery tongue over every little difference or misunderstanding.

A man must begin to wisely control himself, and to learn the beautiful lessons of patience, if he is to be highly prosperous, if he is to be a man of use and power. He must learn to think of others, to act for their good, and not alone for himself; to be considerate, for bearing, and long suffering. He must study how to have a heart at peace with men who differ from him on those things which he regards as most vital. He must avoid quarrelling as he would avoid drinking a deadly poison. Discords from without will be continually overtaking him, but he must fortify himself against them; he must study how to bring harmonies out of them by the exercise of patience.

Strife is common: it pains the heart and distorts the mind. Patience is rare, it enriches the heart and beautifies the mind. Every cat can spit and fume; it requires no effort, but only a looseness of behavior. It takes a man to keep his mornings through all events, and to be painstaking and patient with the shortcomings of humanity. But patience wins. As soft water wears away the hardest rock, so patience overcomes all opposition. It gains the hearts of men. It conquers and controls.

Calmness accompanies patience. It is a great and glorious quality. It is the peaceful haven of emancipated souls after their long wanderings on the tempest riven ocean of passion. It makes the man who has suffered much, endured much, experienced much, and has finally conquered.

A man cannot be impartial who is not calm. Excitement, prejudice, and partiality spring from disturbed passions. When personal feeling is thwarted, it rises and seethes like a stream of water that is dammed. The calm man avoids this disturbance by directing his feeling from the personal to the impersonal channel. He thinks and feels for others as well as for himself. He sets the same value on other men's opinions as on his own. If he regards his on work as important, he sees also that the work of other men is equally important. He does not content for the merit of his own against the demerit of that of others. He is not overthrown, like Humpty dumpty, with a sense of self-importance. He has put aside egotism for truth, and he perceives the right relations of things. He has conquered irritability, and has come to see that there is nothing in itself that should cause irritation. As well be irritable with a pansy because it is not a rose, as a with a man because he does not see as you see. Minds differ, and the calm man recognizes the differences as facts in human nature.

The calm, impartial man, is not only the happiest man, he also has all his powers at his command. He is sure, deliberate, executive, and swiftly and easily accomplishes in silence what the irritable men slowly and laboriously toils through with much nice. His mind is purified, poised, concentrated, and is ready at any moment to be directed upon a given work with unerring power. In the calm mind all contradictions are reconciled, and there is radiant gladness and perpetual peace. As Emerson puts it: "Calmness is joy fixed and habitual".

One should not confound indifference with calmness, for it is at the opposite extreme. Indifference is lifelines, while calmness is glowing life and full orbed power. The calm man has partly or entirely conquered self, and having successfully battled with the selfishness within, he knows how to meet and overcome it successfully in others. In any moral content the calm man is always the victor. So long as he remains calm, defeat is impossible.

Self-control is better than riches and calmness is a perpetual benediction.

Wisdom abides with the impartial man. Her counsels guide him; her wings shield him; she leads him along pleasant ways to happy destinations.

Wisdom is many sided. The wise man adapts himself to others. He acts for their good, yet never violates the moral virtues or the principles of right conduct. The foolish man cannot adapt himself to others; he acts for himself only, and continually violates the moral virtues and the principles of right conduct. There is a degree of wisdom in every act of impartiality, and once a man has touched and experience the impartial zone, he can recover it again and again until he finally establishes himself in it.

Every thought, word, and act of wisdom tells on the world at large, for it is fraught with greatness. Wisdom is a well of knowledge and a spring of power. It is profound and comprehensive, and is so exact and all-inclusive as to embrace the smallest details. In its spacious greatness it does not overlook the small. The wise mind is like the world, it contains all things in their proper place and order, and is not burdened thereby. Like the world also, it is free, and unconscious of any restrictions; yet it is never loose, never erring, never sinful and repentant. Wisdom is the steady, grown up being of whom folly was the crying infant. It was outgrown the weakness and dependence, the errors and punishments of infantile ignorance, and is erect, poised, strong, and serene.

The understanding mind needs no external support. It stands of itself on the firm ground of knowledge; not book-knowledge, but ripened experience. It has passed through all minds, and therefore knows them. It has traveled with all hearts, and knows their journeying in joy and sorrow.

When wisdom touches a man, he is lifted up and transfigured. He becomes a new being with new aims and powers, and he inhabits a new universe in which to accomplish a new and glorious destiny.

Such is the Pillar of impartiality which adds its massive strength and incomparable grace to support and beautify the Temple of Prosperity.

9. Eighth pillar – Self-reliance

Every young man ought to read Emerson's essay on 'Self Reliance.' It is the manliest, most virile essay that was ever penned. It is calculated to cure alike those two mental maladies common to youth, namely, self-depreciation and self-conceit. It is almost as sure to reveal to the prig the smallness and emptiness of his vanity, as it is to show the bashful man the weakness and ineffectuality of his dividence. It is a new revelation of manly dignity; as much a revelation as any that was vouchsafed to ancient seer and prophet, and perhaps a more practical, eminently suited to his mechanic age, coming, as it does from a modern prophet of a new type and called in a new race, and its chief merit is its powerfully tonic quality.

Let not self-reliance be confounded with self-conceit, for as high and excellent as is the one, just so low and worthless is other. There cannot be anything mean in self-reliance, while in self-conceit there cannot be anything great.

The man that never says "no" when questioned on subjects of which he is entirely ignorant, to avoid, as he imagines, being thought ignorant, but confidently puts forward guesses and assumptions as knowledge, will be known for his ignorance, and ill esteemed for his added conceit. An honest confession of ignorance will command respect where a conceited assumption of knowledge will elicit contempt.

The timid, apologetic man who seems almost afraid to live, who fears that he will do something not in the approved way, and will subject himself to ridicule, is not a full man. He must needs imitate others, and have no independent action. He needs that self-reliance which will compel him to fall back on his own initiative, and so become a new example instead of the slavish follower of an old one. As for ridicule he who is hurt by it is no man. The shafts or mockery and sarcasm cannot pierce the strong armour of the self-reliant man. They cannot reach the invincible citadel of his honest heart to sting or wound it. The sharp arrows of irony may rain upon him, but he laughs as they are deflected by the strong breast plate of his confidence, and fall harmless about him.

"Trust thyself," says Emerson, "every heart vibrates to that iron string." Throughout the ages men have so far leaned, and do still lean, upon external makeshifts instead of standing upon their own native simplicity and original dignity. The few who have had the courage to so stand, have been singled out and elevated as heroes; and he is indeed the true hero who has the hardihood to let his nature speak for itself, who has that strong metal which enables him to stand upon his own intrinsic worth.

It is true that the candidate for such heroism must endure the test of strength. He must not be shamed from his ground by the bugbears of an initiate conventionalist. He must not fear for his reputation or position, or for his standing in the church or his prestige in local society. He must learn to act and live as independently of these consideration as he does of the current fashions in the antipodes. Yet when he has endured this test, and stander and odium have failed to move or afflict him, he has become a man indeed, one that society will have to reckon with, and finally accept on his own terms.

Sooner or later all men will turn or guidance to the self-reliant man, and while the best minds do not make a prop of him, they respect and value his work and worth, and recognize his place among the goods that have gone before.

It must not be thought an indication of self-reliance to scorn to learn. Such an attitude is born of a stubborn superciliousness which has the elements of weakness, and is prophetic of a fall, rather than the elements of strength and the promise of high achievement which are characteristic of self-reliance. Pride and vanity must not be associated with self rests upon incidentals and appurtenances – on money, clothing, property, prestige, position and these lost, all is lost. Self reliance rests upon essentials and principles on worth, probity, purity, sincerity, character, truth and whatever may be lost is of little account, for these are never lost. Pride tries to hide its ignorance by ostentation and assumption, and is unwilling to be thought a learner in any direction. It stands, during its little fleeting day, on ignorance and appearance, and the higher it is lifted up today the lower it will be cast down tomorrow. Self reliance has nothing to hide, and is willing to learn; and while there can be no humility where pride is, self-reliance and humility are compatible, nay more, they are complementary, and the sublimes form of self-reliance is only found associated with the profoundest humility. "Extremes meet," says Emerson, "and there is no better example than the haughtiness of humility. No aristocrat, no prince born to the purple, can begin to compare with the self-respect of the saint. Why is he so lowly, but that he knows that he can well afford it, resting on the largeness of God in him?" It was Buddha who said; - "Those who, either now or after I am dead, shall be a lamp unto themselves, relying upon themselves only and not relying upon any external help, but holding fast to the truth as their lamp, and seeking their salvation in the truth alone, shall not look for assistance to any one beside themselves, it is they, among my disciples, who shall reach the very top mist height. But they must be willing to learn." In this saying, the repeated insistence on the necessity for relying upon one's self alone, coupled with the final exhortation to be eager to learn, is the wisest utterance on self-reliance that I know. In it, the Great Teacher comprehends that perfect balance between self-trust and humility which the man of truth must acquire.

"Self-trust is the essence of heroism." All great men are self-reliant, and we should use them as teachers and exemplars and not as props and perambulators. A great man comes who leans upon no one, but stands alone in the solitary dignity of truth, and straightway the world begins to lean upon him, begins to make him an excuse for spiritual indolence and a destructive self-abasement. Better than cradling our vices in the strength of the great would it be to newly light our virtues at their luminous lamp. If we rely upon the light of another, darkness will overtake us, but if we rely upon our own light we have but to keep it burning. We may both draw light from another and communicate it, but to think it sufficient while our own lamp is rusting in neglect, is shortly to find ourselves abandoned in darkness. Our own inner light is the light which never fails us.

What is the "inner light" of the Quakers but another name for self-reliance? We should stand upon what we are, not upon what another is. "But I am so small and poor," you say: well, stand upon that smallness, and presently it will become great. A babe must needs suckle and cling, but not so man. Henceforth he goes upon his own limbs. Men pray to God to put into their hands that which they are framed to reach out for; to put into their mouth the food for which they should strenuously labour. But men will outgrow this spiritual infancy. The time will come when men will no more pay a priest to pray for them and preach to them.

Man's chief trouble is a mistrust of himself, so that the self trusting man becomes a rare and singular spectacle. If a man look upon himself as a "worm," what can come out of him but an ineffectual wriggling. Truly, "He that humbleth shall be exalted," but not he that degradeth himself. A man should see himself as he is, and if there is any unworthiness in him, he should get rid of it, and retain and rely upon that which is of worth. A man is only debased when he debases himself; he is exalted when he lives an exalted life.

Why should a man, with ceaseless iterations, draw attention to his fallen nature? There is a false humility which takes a sort of pride in vice. If one has fallen, it is that he may rise and be the wiser for it. if a man falls into a ditch, he does not lie there and call upon every passerby to mark his fallen state, he gets up and goes on his way with greater care. So if one has fallen into the ditch of vice, let him rise and be cleansed, and go on his way rejoicing.

There is not a sphere in life wherein a man's influence and prosperity will not be considerably increased by even a measure of self-reliance, and to the teacher – whether secular or religious to organizers, managers, overseers, and in all positions of control and command, it is an indispensable equipment.

The four grand qualities of self-reliance are:-

1. Decision
2. Steadfastness
3. Dignity
4. Independence

Decision makes a man strong. The waverer is the weakling. A man who is to play a speaking part, however small, in the drama of life must be decisive and know what he is about. Whatever he doubts, he must not doubt his power to act. He must know his part in life, and put all his energy into it. He must have some solid ground of knowledge from which to work, and stand securely on that. It may be only the price and quality of stock, but he must know his work thoroughly, and know that he knows it. He must be ready at any time to answer for himself when his duty is impugned. He should be so well grounded upon his particular practice as not to be affected with hesitation on any point or in any emergence. It is a true saying that "the man that hesitates is lost." No one believes in him who does not believe in himself, who doubts, halts, and wavers, and cannot extricate himself from the tangled threads of two courses. Who would deal with a tradesman who did not know the price of his own goods, or was not sure where to find them? A man must know his business. If he does not know his own, who shall instruct him? He must be able to give a good report of the truth that is in him, must have that deceive touch which skill and knowledge only can impart.

Certainty is a great element in self-reliance. To have weight, a man must have some truth to impart, and all skill is a communication of truth. He must "speak with authority, and not as the scribes." He must master something, and know that he has mastered it, so as to deal with it lucidly and understandingly, in the way of a master, and not to remain always an apprentice.

Indecision is a disintegrating factor. A minute's faltering may turn back the current of success. Men who are afraid to decide quickly for fear of making a mistake, nearly always makes a mistake when they do act. The quickest, in thought and action, are less liable to blunder, and it is better to act with decision and make a mistake than to act with indecision and make a mistake than to act with indecision and make a mistake, for in the former case there is but error, but in the latter, weakness is added to error.

A man should be decided always, both where he knows and where he does not know. He should be as ready to say "no" as "yes", as quick to acknowledge his ignorance as to impart his knowledge. If he stands upon fact, and acts from the simple truth, he will find no room for halting between two opinions.

Make up your mind quickly, and act decisively. Better still, have a mind that is already made up and then decision will be instinctive and spontaneous.

Steadfastness arises in the mind that is quick to decide. It is indeed a final decision upon the best course of conduct and the best path in life. It is the vow of the soul to stand firmly by its principles whatever betide. It is neither necessary nor unnecessary that there by any written or spoken vow, for unswerving loyalty to a fixed principle is the spirit of all vows.

The man without fixed principles will not accomplish much. Expediency is a quagmire and a thorny waste, in which a man is continually sticking in the shifting mud of his own moral looseness, and is pricked and scratched with the thorns of his self-created disappointments.

One must have some solid ground on which to stand among one's fellows. He cannot stand on the bog of concession. Shiftiness is a vice of weakness, and the vices of weakness do more to undermine character and influence than the vices of strength. The man that is vicious through excess of animal strength takes a shorter cut to truth – when his mind is made up that he who is vicious through lack of virility, and whose chief vice consists in not having a mind of his own upon anything. When one understands that power is adaptable to both good and bad ends, it will not surprise him that the drunkards and harlots should reach the kingdom of heaven before the diplomatic religionists. They are at least through in the course which they have adopted, vile though it be, and thoroughness is strength. It only needs that strength to be turned from bad to good, and lo! The loathed sinner has become the lofty saint!

A man should have a firm, fixed, determined mind. He should decide upon those principles which are best to stand by in all issues, and which will most safely guide him through the maze of conflicting opinions, and inspire him with unflinching courage in the battle of life. Having adopted his principles, they should be more to him than gain or happiness, more even than life itself, and if he never deserts them he will find that they will never desert him; they will defend him from all enemies, deliver him safely from all dangers, light up his pathway through all darkness and difficulties. They will be to him a light in darkness, a resting place from sorrow, and a refuge from the conflicts of the world.

Dignity clothes, as with a majestic garment, the steadfast mind. He who is as unyielding as a bar of steel when he is expected to compromise with evil, and as supple as a willow wand in adapting himself to that which is good, carries about with him a dignity that calms and uplifts others by its presence.

The unsteady mind, the mind that is not anchored to any fixed principles, that is stubborn where its own desires are threatened, and yielding where its own moral welfare is at stake, has no gravity, no balance, no calm composure.

The man of dignity cannot be down-trodden and enslaved, because he has ceased to tread upon and enslave himself. He at once disarms, with a look, a word, a wise and suggestive silence, any attempt to demean him. His mere presence is a wholesome reproof to the flippant and the unseemly, while it is a rock of strength to the lover of the good.

But the chief reason why the dignified man commands respect is, not only that he is supremely self-respecting, but that he graciously treats all others with a due esteem. Pride loves itself, and treats those beneath it with supercilious contempt, for love of self and contempt for others are always found together in equal degrees, so that the greater the self love, the greater the arrogance. True dignity arises, not from self-love, but from self-sacrifice that is, from unbiased adherence to a fixed central principle. The dignity of the Judge arises from the fact that in the performance of his duty he sets aside all personal consideration, and stands solely upon the law; his little personality, impermanent and fleeting' becomes nothing, while the law, enduring and majestic, becomes all. Should a Judge, in deciding a case, forget the law, and fall into personal feeling and prejudice, his dignity would be gone. So with the man of stately purity of character, he stands upon the divine law, and not upon personal feeling, for immediately a man gives way to passion he has sacrificed dignity, and takes his place as one of the multitude of the unwise and uncontrolled.

Every man will have composure and dignity in the measure that he acts from a fixed principle. It only needs that the principle be right, and therefore unassailable. So long as man abides by such a principle, and does not waver or descend into the personal element, attacking passions, prejudices and interests, however powerful, will be weak and ineffectual before the unconquerable strength of an incorruptible principle, and will at last yield their combined and unseemly confusion to his single and majestic right.

Independence is the birthright of the strong and well controlled man. All men love and strive for liberty. All men aspire to some sort of freedom.

A man should labour for himself or for the community. Unless he is a cripple, a chronic invalid, or is mentally irresponsible, he should be ashamed to depend upon others for all he has, giving nothing in return. If one imagines that such a condition is freedom, let him know that it is one of the lowest forms of slavery. The time will come when, to be a drone in the human hive, even (as matters are now) a respectable drone and not a poor tramp, will be a public disgrace, and will be no longer respectable.

Independence, freedom, glorious liberty, come through labour and not from idleness, and the self-reliant man is too strong, too honourable, too upright to depend upon others, like a sucking babe, for his support. He earns, with hand or brain, the right to live as becomes a man and a citizen; and this he does whether born rich or poor, for riches are no excuse for idleness; rather are they an opportunity to labour, with the rare facilities which they afford, for the good of the community.

Only he who is self-supporting is free, self-reliant, independent.

Thus is the nature of the Eight Pillars explained. On what foundation they rest, the manner of their building, their ingredients, the fourfold nature of the material of which each is composed, what positions they occupy, and how they support the Temple, all may now build; and he who knew but imperfectly may know more perfectly; and he who knew perfectly may rejoice in this systematization and simplification of the moral order in Prosperity. Let us now consider the Temple itself, that we may know the might of its Pillars, the strength of its walls, the endurance of its roof, and the architectural beauty and perfection of the whole.

10. The temple of prosperity

The reader who has followed the course of this book with a view to obtaining information on the details of money making, business transactions, profit and loss in various undertakings, prices, markets, agreements, contracts, and other matters connected with the achievement of prosperity, will have noted an entire absence of any instruction on these matters of detail. The reason for this is fourfold, namely:-

First. Details cannot stand alone, but are powerless to build up anything unless intelligently related to principles.

Second. Details are infinite, and are ceaselessly changing, while principles are few, and are eternal and unchangeable.

Third. Principles are the coherent factors in all details, regulating and harmonizing them, so that to have right principles is to be right in all the subsidiary details.

Fourth. A teacher of truth in any direction must adhere rigidly to principles, and must not allow himself to be drawn away from them into the ever-changing maze of private particulars and personal details, because such particulars and details have only a local right, and are only necessary for certain individuals, while principles are universally right and are necessary for all men.

He who grasps the principles of this book so as to be able to intelligently practice them, will be able to reach the heart of this fourfold reason. The details of a man's affairs are important, but they are his details or the details of his particular branch of industry, and all outside that branch are not concerned with them, but moral principles are the same for all men; they are applicable to all conditions, and govern all particulars.

The man who works from fixed principles does not need to harass himself over the complications of numerous details. He will grasp, as it were, the entire details in one single thought, and will see them through and through, illumined by the light of the principle to which they stand related, and this without friction, and with freedom from anxiety and strain.

Until principles are grasped, details are regarded, and dealt with, as primary matters, and so viewed they lead to innumerable complications and confused issues. In the light of principles, they are seen to be secondary facts, and so seen, all difficulties connected with them are at once overcome and annulled by a reference to principles.

He who is involved in numerous details without the regulating and synthesizing element of principles is like one lost in a forest, with no direct path along which to walk amid the mass of objects. He is swelled up by the details, while the man of principles contains all details within himself; he stands outside them, as it were, and grasps them in their entirety, while the other man can only see the few that are nearest to him at the time.

All things are contained in principles. They are the laws of things, and all things observe their own law. It is an error to view things apart from their nature. Details are the letter of which principles are the spirit. It is as true in art, science, literature, commerce, as in religion, that "the letter killeth, the spirit of giveth life." The body of a man, with its wonderful combination of parts, is important, but only in its relation to the spirit. The spirit being withdrawn, the body is useless and is put away. The body of a business, with all its complicated details is important, but only in its relation to the vivifying principles by which it is controlled. These withdrawn, the business will perish.

To have the body of prosperity – its material presentation – we must first have the spirit of prosperity, and the spirit of prosperity is the quick spirit of moral virtue. Moral blindness prevails. Men see money, property, pleasure, leisure, etc., and, mistaking them for prosperity, strive to get them for their own enjoyment, but, when obtained, they find no enjoyment in them.

Prosperity is at first a spirit, an attitude of mind, a moral power, a life, which manifests outwardly in the form of plenty, happiness, joy. Just as a man cannot become a genius by writing poems, essay as plays, but must develop and acquire the soul of genius – when the writing will follow as effect to cause-so one cannot become prosperous by hoarding up money, and by gaining property and possessions, but must develop and acquire the soul of virtue, when the material accessories will follow as effect to cause, for the spirit of virtue is the spirit of joy, and it contains within itself all abundance, all satisfaction, all fullness of life.

There is no joy in money, there is no joy in property, there is no joy in material accumulations or in any material things of itself. These things are dead and lifeless. The spirit of joy must be in the man or it is nowhere. He must have within him the capacity for happiness. He must have the wisdom to know how to use these things, and not merely hoard them. He must possess them, and not be possessed by them. They must be dependent upon him, and not he upon them. They must be dependent upon him, and not he upon them. They must follow him, and not be for ever be running after them; and they will inevitably follow him, if he has the moral elements within to which they are related.

Nothing is absent from the Kingdom of heaven; it contains all good, true, and necessary things, and "the Kingdom of God is within you." I know rich people who are supremely happy, because they are generous, magnanimous, pure and joyful; but I also know rich people who are very miserable, and these are they who looked to money and possessions for their happiness, and have not developed the spirit of good and of joy within themselves.

How can it be said of a wretched man that he is "prosperous", even if his income be ten thousand pounds a year? There must be fitness, and harmony, and satisfaction in a true prosperity. When a rich man is happy, it is that he brought the spirit of happiness to his riches, and not that the riches brought happiness to him. He is a full man with full material advantages and responsibilities, while the miserable rich man is an empty man looking to riches for that fullness of life which can only be evolved from within.

Thus prosperity resolves itself into a moral capacity, and in the wisdom to rightfully use and lawfully enjoy the material things which are inseparable from our earthly life. If one would be free without, let him first be free within, for if he be bound in a spirit by weakness, selfishness, or vice, how can the possession of money liberate him! Will it not rather become, in his hands, a ready instrument by which to further enslave himself?

The visible effects of prosperity, then, must not be considered alone, but in their relation to the mental and moral cause. There is a hidden foundation to every building; the fact that it continues to stands is proof of that. There is a hidden foundation to every from of established success; its permanence proves that it is so. Prosperity stands on the foundation of character, and there is not, in all the wide universe, any other foundation. True wealth is weal, welfare, well-being, soundness, wholeness, and happiness. The wretched rich are not truly wealthy. They are merely encumbered with money, luxury, and leisure, as instruments of self torture. By their possessions they are self cursed.

The moral man is ever blessed, ever happy, and his life, viewed as a whole, is always a success. To these there is no exception, for whatever failures he may have in detail, the finished work of his life will be sound, whole, complete; and through all he will have a quiet conscience, an honorable name, and all manifold blessings which are inseparable from richness of character, and without this moral richness, financial riches will not avail or satisfy.

Let us briefly recapitulate, and again view the Eight Pillars in their strength and splendour.

Energy – Rousing one's self up to strenuous and unremitting exertion in the accomplishment of one's task.

Economy – Concentration of power, the conservation of both capital and character, the latter being mental capital, and therefore of the utmost importance.

Integrity – Unswerving honesty; keeping inviolate all promises, agreements, and contracts, apart from all considerations of loss or gain.

System – Making all details, subservient to order, and thereby relieving the memory and the mind of superfluous work and strain by reducing many to one.

Sympathy – Magnanimity, generosity, gentleness, and tenderness; being open handed, free, and kind.

Sincerity – Being sound and whole, robust and true; and therefore not being one person in public and another in private, and not assuming good actions openly while doing bad actions in secret.

Impartiality – Justice; not striving for self, but weighing both sides, and acting in accordance with equity.

Self – Reliance – Looking to one's self only for strength and support by standing on principles which are fixed and invincible, and not relying upon outward things which at any moment may be snatched away.

How can any life be other than successful which is built on these Eight Pillars? Their strength is such that no physical or intellectual strength can compare with it; and to have built all the eight perfectly would render a man invincible. It will be found, however, that men are often strong in one or several of these qualities, and weak in others, and it is this weak element that invites failure. It is foolish, for instance, to attribute a man's failure in business to his honest. It is impossible for honesty to produce failure. The cause of failure must be looked for in some other direction – in the lack, and not the possession, of some good necessary quality. Moreover, such attribution of failure to honesty is a slur on the integrity of commerce; and a false indictment of those men, numerous enough, who are honourably engaged in trade. A man may be strong in Energy, Economy, and System, but comparatively weak in the other five. Such a man will just fail of complete success by lacking one of the four corner pillars, namely, Integrity. His temple will give way at that weak corner, for the first four Pillars must be well built before the Temple of Prosperity can stand secure. They are the first qualities to be acquired in a man's moral evolution, and without them the second four cannot be possessed. Again, if a man be strong in the first three, and lack the fourth, the absence of order will invite confusion and disaster into his affairs; and so on with any partial combination of these qualities, especially of the first four, for the second four are of so lofty a character that at present men can but possess them, with rare exceptions, in a more or less imperfect form. The man of the world, then, who wishes to secure an abiding success in any branch of commerce, or in one of the many lines of industry in which men are commonly engaged, must build into his character, by practice, the first four moral Pillars. By these fixed principles he must regulate his thought, his conduct, and his affairs; consulting them in every difficulty, making every detail serve them, and above all, never deserting them under any circumstance to gain some personal advantage or to save some personal trouble, for to so desert them is to make one's self vulnerable to the disintegrating elements of evil, and to become assailable to accusations from others. He who so abides by these four principles will achieve a full measure of success in his own particular work, whatever it may be; his Temple of Prosperity will be well built and well supported, and it will stand secure. The perfect practice of these four principles is within the scope of all men who are willing to study them with that object in view, for they are so simple and plain that a child could grasp their meaning, and their perfection in conduct does not call for an unusual degree of self-sacrifice, though it demands some self-denial and personal discipline without which there can be no success in this world of action. The second four pillars, however, are principles of a more profound nature, are more difficult to understand and practice, and call from the highest degree of self-sacrifice and self-effacement. Few, at present, can reach that detachment from the personal element which their perfect practice demands, but the few who accomplish this in any marked degree will vastly enlarge their powers and enrich their life, and will adorn their Temple of Prosperity with a singular and attractive beauty which will gladden and elevate all beholders long after they have passed away.

But those who are beginning to build their Temple of Prosperity in accordance with the teaching of this book, must bear in mind that a building requires time to erect, and it must be patiently raised up, brick upon brick and stone upon stone, and the Pillars must be firmly fixed and cemented, and labour and care will be needed to make the whole complete. And the building of this inner mental Temple is none the less real and substantial because invisible and noiseless, for in the raising up of his, as of Solomon's Temple which was "seven years in building" – it can be said, "there was neither hammer nor axe nor any tool of iron heard in the house, while it was in the building".

Even so, oh reader construct thy character, raise up the house of thy life, build up thy Temple of Prosperity. Be not as the foolish who rise and fall upon the uncertain flux of selfish desires: but be at peace in thy labour, crown thy career with completeness, and so be numbered among the wise who, without uncertainty, build upon a fixed and secure foundation – even upon the Principles of Truth which endure for ever.

The Way of Peace

The Power of Meditation

Spiritual meditation is the pathway to Divinity. It is the mystic ladder which reaches from earth to heaven, from error to Truth, from pain to peace. Every saint has climbed it; every sinner must sooner or later come to it, and every weary pilgrim that turns his back upon self and the world, and sets his face resolutely toward the Father's Home, must plant his feet upon its golden rounds. Without its aid you cannot grow into the divine state, the divine likeness, the divine peace, and the fadeless glories and unpolluting joys of Truth will remain hidden from you.

Meditation is the intense dwelling, in thought, upon an idea or theme, with the object of thoroughly comprehending it, and whatsoever you constantly meditate upon you will not only come to understand, but will grow more and more into its likeness, for it will become incorporated into your very being, will become, in fact, your very self. If, therefore, you constantly dwell upon that which is selfish and debasing, you will ultimately become selfish and debased; if you ceaselessly think upon that which is pure and unselfish you will surely become pure and unselfish.

Tell me what that is upon which you most frequently and intensely think, that to which, in your silent hours, your soul most naturally turns, and I will tell you to what place of pain or peace you are traveling, and whether you are growing into the likeness of the divine or the bestial.

There is an unavoidable tendency to become literally the embodiment of that quality upon which one most constantly thinks. Let, therefore, the object of your meditation be above and not below, so that every time you revert to it in thought you will be lifted up; let it be pure and unmixed with any selfish element; so shall your heart become purified and drawn nearer to Truth, and not defiled and dragged more hopelessly into error.

Meditation, in the spiritual sense in which I am now using it, is the secret of all growth in spiritual life and knowledge. Every prophet, sage, and savior became such by the power of meditation. Buddha meditated upon the Truth until he could say, "I am the Truth." Jesus brooded upon the Divine immanence until at last he could declare, "I and my Father are One."

Meditation centered upon divine realities is the very essence and soul of prayer. It is the silent reaching of the soul toward the Eternal. Mere petitionary prayer without meditation is a body without a soul, and is powerless to lift the mind and heart above sin and affliction. If you are daily praying for wisdom, for peace, for loftier purity and a fuller realization of Truth, and that for which you pray is still far from you, it means that you are praying for one thing while living out in thought and act another. If you will cease from such waywardness, taking your mind off those things the selfish clinging to which debars you from the possession of the stainless realities for which you pray: if you will no longer ask God to grant you that which you do not deserve, or to bestow upon you that love and compassion which you refuse to bestow upon others, but will commence to think and act in the spirit of Truth, you will day by day be growing into those realities, so that ultimately you will become one with them.

He who would secure any worldly advantage must be willing to work vigorously for it, and he would be foolish indeed who, waiting with folded hands, expected it to come to him for the mere asking. Do not then vainly imagine that you can obtain the heavenly possessions without making an effort. Only when you commence to work earnestly in the Kingdom of Truth will you be allowed to partake of the Bread of Life, and when you have, by patient and uncomplaining effort, earned the spiritual wages for which you ask, they will not be withheld from you.

If you really seek Truth, and not merely your own gratification; if you love it above all worldly pleasures and gains; more, even, than happiness itself, you will be willing to make the effort necessary for its achievement.

If you would be freed from sin and sorrow; if you would taste of that spotless purity for which you sigh and pray; if you would realize wisdom and knowledge, and would enter into the possession of profound and abiding peace, come now and enter the path of meditation, and let the supreme object of your meditation be Truth.

At the outset, meditation must be distinguished from idle reverie. There is nothing dreamy and unpractical about it. It is a process of searching and uncompromising thought which allows nothing to remain but the simple and naked truth. Thus meditating you will no longer strive to build yourself up in your prejudices, but, forgetting self, you will remember only that you are seeking the Truth. And so you will remove, one by one, the errors which you have built around yourself in the past, and will patiently wait for the revelation of Truth which will come when your errors have been sufficiently removed. In the silent humility of your heart you will realize that

"There is an inmost centre in us all
Where Truth abides in fulness; and around,
Wall upon wall, the gross flesh hems it in;
This perfect, clear perception, which is Truth,

A baffling and perverting carnal mesh
Blinds it, and makes all error; and to know,
Rather consists in opening out a way
Whence the imprisoned splendour may escape,
Than in effecting entry for a light
Supposed to be without."

Select some portion of the day in which to meditate, and keep that period sacred to your purpose. The best time is the very early morning when the spirit of repose is upon everything. All natural conditions will then be in your favor; the passions, after the long bodily fast of the night, will be subdued, the excitements and worries of the previous day will have died away, and the mind, strong and yet restful, will be receptive to spiritual instruction. Indeed, one of the first efforts you will be called upon to make will be to shake off lethargy and indulgence, and if you refuse you will be unable to advance, for the demands of the spirit are imperative.

To be spiritually awakened is also to be mentally and physically awakened. The sluggard and the self-indulgent can have no knowledge of Truth. He who, possessed of health and strength, wastes the calm, precious hours of the silent morning in drowsy indulgence is totally unfit to climb the heavenly heights.

He whose awakening consciousness has become alive to its lofty possibilities, who is beginning to shake off the darkness of ignorance in which the world is enveloped, rises before the stars have ceased their vigil, and, grappling with the darkness within his soul, strives, by holy aspiration, to perceive the light of Truth while the unawakened world dreams on.

"The heights by great men reached and kept,
Were not attained by sudden flight,
But they, while their companions slept,
Were toiling upward in the night."

No saint, no holy man, no teacher of Truth ever lived who did not rise early in the morning. Jesus habitually rose early, and climbed the solitary mountains to engage in holy communion. Buddha always rose an hour before sunrise and engaged in meditation, and all his disciples were enjoined to do the same.

If you have to commence your daily duties at a very early hour, and are thus debarred from giving the early morning to systematic meditation, try to give an hour at night, and should this, by the length and laboriousness of your daily task be denied you, you need not despair, for you may turn your thoughts upward in holy meditation in the intervals of your work, or in those few idle minutes which you now waste in aimlessness; and should your work be of that kind which becomes by practice automatic, you may meditate while engaged upon it. That eminent Christian saint and philosopher, Jacob Boehme, realized his vast knowledge of divine things whilst working long hours as a shoemaker. In every life there is time to think, and the busiest, the most laborious is not shut out from aspiration and meditation.

Spiritual meditation and self-discipline are inseparable; you will, therefore, commence to meditate upon yourself so as to try and understand yourself, for, remember, the great object you will have in view will be the complete removal of all your errors in order that you may realize Truth. You will begin to question your motives, thoughts, and acts, comparing them with your ideal, and endeavoring to look upon them with a calm and impartial eye. In this manner you will be continually gaining more of that mental and spiritual equilibrium without which men are but helpless straws upon the ocean of life. If you are given to hatred or anger you will meditate upon gentleness and forgiveness, so as to become acutely alive to a sense of your harsh and foolish conduct. You will then begin to dwell in thoughts of love, of gentleness, of abounding forgiveness; and as you overcome the lower by the higher, there will gradually, silently steal into your heart a knowledge of the divine Law of Love with an understanding of its bearing upon all the intricacies of life and conduct. And in applying this knowledge to your every thought, word, and act, you will grow more and more gentle, more and more loving, more and more divine. And thus with every error, every selfish desire, every human weakness; by the power of meditation is it overcome, and as each sin, each error is thrust out, a fuller and clearer measure of the Light of Truth illumines the pilgrim soul.

Thus meditating, you will be ceaselessly fortifying yourself against your only real enemy, your selfish, perishable self, and will be establishing yourself more and more firmly in the divine and imperishable self that is inseparable from Truth. The direct outcome of your meditations will be a calm, spiritual strength which will be your stay and resting-place in the struggle of life. Great is the overcoming power of holy thought, and the strength and knowledge gained in the hour of silent meditation will enrich the soul with saving remembrance in the hour of strife, of sorrow, or of temptation.

As, by the power of meditation, you grow in wisdom, you will relinquish, more and more, your selfish desires which are fickle, impermanent, and productive of sorrow and pain; and will take your stand, with increasing steadfastness and trust, upon unchangeable principles, and will realize heavenly rest.

The use of meditation is the acquirement of a knowledge of eternal principles, and the power which results from meditation is the ability to rest upon and trust those principles, and so become one with the Eternal. The end of meditation is, therefore, direct knowledge of Truth, God, and the realization of divine and profound peace.

Let your meditations take their rise from the ethical ground which you now occupy. Remember that you are to grow into Truth by steady perseverance. If you are an orthodox Christian, meditate ceaselessly upon the spotless purity and divine excellence of the character of Jesus, and apply his every precept to your inner life and outward conduct, so as to approximate more and more toward his perfection. Do not be as those religious ones, who, refusing to meditate upon the Law of Truth, and to put into practice the precepts given to them by their Master, are content to formally worship, to cling to their particular creeds, and to continue in the ceaseless round of sin and suffering. Strive to rise, by the power of meditation, above all selfish clinging to partial gods or party creeds; above dead formalities and lifeless ignorance. Thus walking the high way of wisdom, with mind fixed upon the spotless Truth, you shall know no halting-place short of the realization of Truth.

He who earnestly meditates first perceives a truth, as it were, afar off, and then realizes it by daily practice. It is only the doer of the Word of Truth that can know of the doctrine of Truth, for though by pure thought the Truth is perceived, it is only actualized by practice.

Said the divine Gautama, the Buddha, "He who gives himself up to vanity, and does not give himself up to meditation, forgetting the real aim of life and grasping at pleasure, will in time envy him who has exerted himself in meditation," and he instructed his disciples in the following "Five Great Meditations":—

"The first meditation is the meditation of love, in which you so adjust your heart that you long for the weal and welfare of all beings, including the happiness of your enemies.

"The second meditation is the meditation of pity, in which you think of all beings in distress, vividly representing in your imagination their sorrows and anxieties so as to arouse a deep compassion for them in your soul.

"The third meditation is the meditation of joy, in which you think of the prosperity of others, and rejoice with their rejoicings.

"The fourth meditation is the meditation of impurity, in which you consider the evil consequences of corruption, the effects of sin and diseases. How trivial often the pleasure of the moment, and how fatal its consequences.

"The fifth meditation is the meditation on serenity, in which you rise above love and hate, tyranny and oppression, wealth and want, and regard your own fate with impartial calmness and perfect tranquillity."

By engaging in these meditations the disciples of the Buddha arrived at a knowledge of the Truth. But whether you engage in these particular meditations or not matters little so long as your object is Truth, so long as you hunger and thirst for that righteousness which is a holy heart and a blameless life. In your meditations, therefore, let your heart grow and expand with ever-broadening love, until, freed from all hatred, and passion, and condemnation, it embraces the whole universe with thoughtful tenderness. As the flower opens its petals to receive the morning light, so open your soul more and more to the glorious light of Truth. Soar upward upon the wings of aspiration; be fearless, and believe in the loftiest possibilities. Believe that a life of absolute meekness is possible; believe that a life of stainless purity is possible; believe that a life of perfect holiness is possible; believe that the realization of the highest truth is possible. He who so believes, climbs rapidly the heavenly hills, whilst the unbelievers continue to grope darkly and painfully in the fog-bound valleys.

So believing, so aspiring, so meditating, divinely sweet and beautiful will be your spiritual experiences, and glorious the revelations that will enrapture your inward vision. As you realize the divine Love, the divine Justice, the divine Purity, the Perfect Law of Good, or God, great will be your bliss and deep your peace. Old things will pass away, and all things will become new. The veil of the material universe, so dense and impenetrable to the eye of error, so thin and gauzy to the eye of Truth, will be lifted and the spiritual universe will be revealed. Time will cease, and you will live only in Eternity. Change and mortality will no more cause you anxiety and sorrow, for you will become established in the unchangeable, and will dwell in the very heart of immortality.

Star of Wisdom

Star that of the birth of Vishnu,
Birth of Krishna, Buddha, Jesus,
Told the wise ones, Heavenward looking,
Waiting, watching for thy gleaming
In the darkness of the night-time,
In the starless gloom of midnight;
Shining Herald of the coming
Of the kingdom of the righteous;
Teller of the Mystic story

Of the lowly birth of Godhead
In the stable of the passions,
In the manger of the mind-soul;
Silent singer of the secret
Of compassion deep and holy
To the heart with sorrow burdened,
To the soul with waiting weary:—
Star of all-surpassing brightness,
Thou again dost deck the midnight;
Thou again dost cheer the wise ones
Watching in the creedal darkness,
Weary of the endless battle
With the grinding blades of error;
Tired of lifeless, useless idols,
Of the dead forms of religions;
Spent with watching for thy shining;
Thou hast ended their despairing;
Thou hast lighted up their pathway;
Thou hast brought again the old Truths
To the hearts of all thy Watchers;
To the souls of them that love thee
Thou dost speak of Joy and Gladness,
Of the peace that comes of Sorrow.
Blessed are they that can see thee,
Weary wanderers in the Night-time;
Blessed they who feel the throbbing,
In their bosoms feel the pulsing
Of a deep Love stirred within them
By the great power of thy shining.
Let us learn thy lesson truly;
Learn it faithfully and humbly;
Learn it meekly, wisely, gladly,
Ancient Star of holy Vishnu,
Light of Krishna, Buddha, Jesus.
The two Masters, Self and Truth

Upon the battlefield of the human soul two masters are ever contending for the crown of supremacy, for the kingship and dominion of the heart; the master of self, called also the "Prince of this world," and the master of Truth, called also the Father God. The master self is that rebellious one whose weapons are passion, pride, avarice, vanity, self-will, implements of darkness; the master Truth is that meek and lowly one whose weapons are gentleness, patience, purity, sacrifice, humility, love, instruments of Light.

In every soul the battle is waged, and as a soldier cannot engage at once in two opposing armies, so every heart is enlisted either in the ranks of self or of Truth. There is no half-and-half course; "There is self and there is Truth; where self is, Truth is not, where Truth is, self is not." Thus spake Buddha, the teacher of Truth, and Jesus, the manifested Christ, declared that "No man can serve two masters; for either he will hate the one and love the other; or else he will hold to the one, and despise the other. Ye cannot serve God and Mammon."

Truth is so simple, so absolutely undeviating and uncompromising that it admits of no complexity, no turning, no qualification. Self is ingenious, crooked, and, governed by subtle and snaky desire, admits of endless turnings and qualifications, and the deluded worshipers of self vainly imagine that they can gratify every worldly desire, and at the same time possess the Truth. But the lovers of Truth worship Truth with the sacrifice of self, and ceaselessly guard themselves against worldliness and self-seeking.

Do you seek to know and to realize Truth? Then you must be prepared to sacrifice, to renounce to the uttermost, for Truth in all its glory can only be perceived and known when the last vestige of self has disappeared.

The eternal Christ declared that he who would be His disciple must "deny himself daily." Are you willing to deny yourself, to give up your lusts, your prejudices, your opinions? If so, you may enter the narrow way of Truth, and find that peace from which the world is shut out. The absolute denial, the utter extinction, of self is the perfect state of Truth, and all religions and philosophies are but so many aids to this supreme attainment.

Self is the denial of Truth. Truth is the denial of self. As you let self die, you will be reborn in Truth. As you cling to self, Truth will be hidden from you.

Whilst you cling to self, your path will be beset with difficulties, and repeated pains, sorrows, and disappointments will be your lot. There are no difficulties in Truth, and coming to Truth, you will be freed from all sorrow and disappointment.

Truth in itself is not hidden and dark. It is always revealed and is perfectly transparent. But the blind and wayward self cannot perceive it. The light of day is not hidden except to the blind, and the Light of Truth is not hidden except to those who are blinded by self.

Truth is the one Reality in the universe, the inward Harmony, the perfect Justice, the eternal Love. Nothing can be added to it, nor taken from it. It does not depend upon any man, but all men depend upon it. You cannot perceive the beauty of Truth while you are looking out through the eyes of self. If you are vain, you will color everything with your own vanities. If lustful, your heart and mind will be so clouded with the smoke and flames of passion, that everything will appear distorted through them. If proud and opinionative, you will see nothing in the whole universe except the magnitude and importance of your own opinions.

There is one quality which pre-eminently distinguishes the man of Truth from the man of self, and that is humility. To be not only free from vanity, stubbornness and egotism, but to regard one's own opinions as of no value, this indeed is true humility.

He who is immersed in self regards his own opinions as Truth, and the opinions of other men as error. But that humble Truth-lover who has learned to distinguish between opinion and Truth, regards all men with the eye of charity, and does not seek to defend his opinions against theirs, but sacrifices those opinions that he may love the more, that he may manifest the spirit of Truth, for Truth in its very nature is ineffable and can only be lived. He who has most of charity has most of Truth.

Men engage in heated controversies, and foolishly imagine they are defending the Truth, when in reality they are merely defending their own petty interests and perishable opinions. The follower of self takes up arms against others. The follower of Truth takes up arms against himself. Truth, being unchangeable and eternal, is independent of your opinion and of mine. We may enter into it, or we may stay outside; but both our defense and our attack are superfluous, and are hurled back upon ourselves.

Men, enslaved by self, passionate, proud, and condemnatory, believe their particular creed or religion to be the Truth, and all other religions to be error; and they proselytize with passionate ardor. There is but one religion, the religion of Truth. There is but one error, the error of self. Truth is not a formal belief; it is an unselfish, holy, and aspiring heart, and he who has Truth is at peace with all, and cherishes all with thoughts of love.

You may easily know whether you are a child of Truth or a worshiper of self, if you will silently examine your mind, heart, and conduct. Do you harbor thoughts of suspicion, enmity, envy, lust, pride, or do you strenuously fight against these? If the former, you are chained to self, no matter what religion you may profess; if the latter, you are a candidate for Truth, even though outwardly you may profess no religion. Are you passionate, self-willed, ever seeking to gain your own ends, self-indulgent, and self-centered; or are you gentle, mild, unselfish, quit of every form of self-indulgence, and are ever ready to give up your own? If the former, self is your master; if the latter, Truth is the object of your affection. Do you strive for riches? Do you fight, with passion, for your party? Do you lust for power and leadership? Are you given to ostentation and self-praise? Or have you given up the love of riches? Have you relinquished all strife? Are you content to take the lowest place, and to be passed by unnoticed? And have you ceased to talk about yourself and to regard yourself with self-complacent pride? If the former, even though you may imagine you worship God, the god of your heart is self. If the latter, even though you may withhold your lips from worship, you are dwelling with the Most High.

The signs by which the Truth-lover is known are unmistakable. Hear the Holy Krishna declare them, in Sir Edwin Arnold's beautiful rendering of the Bhagavad Gita:—

"Fearlessness, singleness of soul, the will
Always to strive for wisdom; opened hand
And governed appetites; and piety,
And love of lonely study; humbleness,
Uprightness, heed to injure nought which lives
Truthfulness, slowness unto wrath, a mind
That lightly letteth go what others prize;
And equanimity, and charity
Which spieth no man's faults; and tenderness
Towards all that suffer; a contented heart,
Fluttered by no desires; a bearing mild,
Modest and grave, with manhood nobly mixed,
With patience, fortitude and purity;
An unrevengeful spirit, never given
To rate itself too high—such be the signs,
O Indian Prince! of him whose feet are set
On that fair path which leads to heavenly birth!"

When men, lost in the devious ways of error and self, have forgotten the "heavenly birth," the state of holiness and Truth, they set up artificial standards by which to judge one another, and make acceptance of, and adherence to, their own particular theology, the test of Truth; and so men are divided one against another, and there is ceaseless enmity and strife, and unending sorrow and suffering.

Reader, do you seek to realize the birth into Truth? There is only one way: Let self die. All those lusts, appetites, desires, opinions, limited conceptions and prejudices to which you have hitherto so tenaciously clung, let them fall from you. Let them no longer hold you in bondage, and Truth will be yours. Cease to look upon your own religion as superior to all others, and strive humbly to learn the supreme lesson of charity. No longer cling to the idea, so productive of strife and sorrow, that the Savior whom you worship is the only Savior, and that the Savior whom your brother worships with equal sincerity and ardor, is an impostor; but seek diligently the path of holiness, and then you will realize that every holy man is a savior of mankind.

The giving up of self is not merely the renunciation of outward things. It consists of the renunciation of the inward sin, the inward error. Not by giving up vain clothing; not by relinquishing riches; not by abstaining from certain foods; not by speaking smooth words; not by merely doing these things is the Truth found; but by giving up the spirit of vanity; by relinquishing the desire for riches; by abstaining from the lust of self-indulgence; by giving up all hatred, strife, condemnation, and self-seeking, and becoming gentle and pure at heart; by doing these things is the Truth found. To do the former, and not to do the latter, is pharisaism and hypocrisy, whereas the latter includes the former. You may renounce the outward world, and isolate yourself in a cave or in the depths of a forest, but you will take all your selfishness with you, and unless you renounce that, great indeed will be your wretchedness and deep your delusion. You may remain just where you are, performing all your duties, and yet renounce the world, the inward enemy. To be in the world and yet not of the world is the highest perfection, the most blessed peace, is to achieve the greatest victory. The renunciation of self is the way of Truth, therefore,

"Enter the Path; there is no grief like hate,
No pain like passion, no deceit like sense;
Enter the Path; far hath he gone whose foot
Treads down one fond offense."

As you succeed in overcoming self you will begin to see things in their right relations. He who is swayed by any passion, prejudice, like or dislike, adjusts everything to that particular bias, and sees only his own delusions. He who is absolutely free from all passion, prejudice, preference, and partiality, sees himself as he is; sees others as they are; sees all things in their proper proportions and right relations. Having nothing to attack, nothing to defend, nothing to conceal, and no interests to guard, he is at peace. He has realized the profound simplicity of Truth, for this unbiased, tranquil, blessed state of mind and heart is the state of Truth. He who attains to it dwells with the angels, and sits at the footstool of the Supreme. Knowing the Great Law; knowing the origin of sorrow; knowing the secret of suffering; knowing the way of emancipation in Truth, how can such a one engage in strife or condemnation; for though he knows that the blind, self-seeking world, surrounded with the clouds of its own illusions, and enveloped in the darkness of error and self, cannot perceive the steadfast Light of Truth, and is utterly incapable of comprehending the profound simplicity of the heart that has died, or is dying, to self, yet he also knows that when the suffering ages have piled up mountains of sorrow, the crushed and burdened soul of the world will fly to its final refuge, and that when the ages are completed, every prodigal will come back to the fold of Truth. And so he dwells in goodwill toward all, and regards all with that tender compassion which a father bestows upon his wayward children.

Men cannot understand Truth because they cling to self, because they believe in and love self, because they believe self to be the only reality, whereas it is the one delusion.

When you cease to believe in and love self you will desert it, and will fly to Truth, and will find the eternal Reality.

When men are intoxicated with the wines of luxury, and pleasure, and vanity, the thirst of life grows and deepens within them, and they delude themselves with dreams of fleshly immortality, but when they come to reap the harvest of their own sowing, and pain and sorrow supervene, then, crushed and humiliated, relinquishing self and all the intoxications of self, they come, with aching hearts to the one immortality, the immortality that destroys all delusions, the spiritual immortality in Truth.

Men pass from evil to good, from self to Truth, through the dark gate of sorrow, for sorrow and self are inseparable. Only in the peace and bliss of Truth is all sorrow vanquished. If you suffer disappointment because your cherished plans have been thwarted, or because someone has not come up to your anticipations, it is because you are clinging to self. If you suffer remorse for your conduct, it is because you have given way to self. If you are overwhelmed with chagrin and regret because of the attitude of someone else toward you, it is because you have been cherishing self. If you are wounded on account of what has been done to you or said of you, it is because you are walking in the painful way of self. All suffering is of self. All suffering ends in Truth. When you have entered into and realized Truth, you will no longer suffer disappointment, remorse, and regret, and sorrow will flee from you.

"Self is the only prison that can ever bind the soul;
Truth is the only angel that can bid the gates unroll;
And when he comes to call thee, arise and follow fast;
His way may lie through darkness, but it leads to light at last."

The woe of the world is of its own making. Sorrow purifies and deepens the soul, and the extremity of sorrow is the prelude to Truth.

Have you suffered much? Have you sorrowed deeply? Have you pondered seriously upon the problem of life? If so, you are prepared to wage war against self, and to become a disciple of Truth.

The intellectual who do not see the necessity for giving up self, frame endless theories about the universe, and call them Truth; but do thou pursue that direct line of conduct which is the practice of righteousness, and thou wilt realize the Truth which has no place in theory, and which never changes. Cultivate your heart. Water it continually with unselfish love and deep-felt pity, and strive to shut out from it all thoughts and feelings which are not in accordance with Love. Return good for evil, love for hatred, gentleness for ill-treatment, and remain silent when attacked. So shall you transmute all your selfish desires into the pure gold of Love, and self will disappear in Truth. So will you walk blamelessly among men, yoked with the easy yoke of lowliness, and clothed with the divine garment of humility.

O come, weary brother! thy struggling and striving
End thou in the heart of the Master of ruth;
Across self's drear desert why wilt thou be driving,
Athirst for the quickening waters of Truth

When here, by the path of thy searching and sinning,
Flows Life's gladsome stream, lies Love's oasis green?
Come, turn thou and rest; know the end and beginning,
The sought and the searcher, the seer and seen.

Thy Master sits not in the unapproached mountains,
Nor dwells in the mirage which floats on the air,
Nor shalt thou discover His magical fountains
In pathways of sand that encircle despair.

In selfhood's dark desert cease wearily seeking
The odorous tracks of the feet of thy King;
And if thou wouldst hear the sweet sound of His speaking,
Be deaf to all voices that emptily sing.

Flee the vanishing places; renounce all thou hast;
Leave all that thou lovest, and, naked and bare,
Thyself at the shrine of the Innermost cast;
The Highest, the Holiest, the Changeless is there.

Within, in the heart of the Silence He dwelleth;

Leave sorrow and sin, leave thy wanderings sore;
Come bathe in His Joy, whilst He, whispering, telleth
Thy soul what it seeketh, and wander no more.

Then cease, weary brother, thy struggling and striving;
Find peace in the heart of the Master of ruth.
Across self's dark desert cease wearily driving;
Come; drink at the beautiful waters of Truth.

The Acquirement of Spiritual Power

The world is filled with men and women seeking pleasure, excitement, novelty; seeking ever to be moved to laughter or tears; not seeking strength, stability, and power; but courting weakness, and eagerly engaged in dispersing what power they have.

Men and women of real power and influence are few, because few are prepared to make the sacrifice necessary to the acquirement of power, and fewer still are ready to patiently build up character.

To be swayed by your fluctuating thoughts and impulses is to be weak and powerless; to rightly control and direct those forces is to be strong and powerful. Men of strong animal passions have much of the ferocity of the beast, but this is not power. The elements of power are there; but it is only when this ferocity is tamed and subdued by the higher intelligence that real power begins; and men can only grow in power by awakening themselves to higher and ever higher states of intelligence and consciousness.

The difference between a man of weakness and one of power lies not in the strength of the personal will (for the stubborn man is usually weak and foolish), but in that focus of consciousness which represents their states of knowledge.

The pleasure-seekers, the lovers of excitement, the hunters after novelty, and the victims of impulse and hysterical emotion lack that knowledge of principles which gives balance, stability, and influence.

A man commences to develop power when, checking his impulses and selfish inclinations, he falls back upon the higher and calmer consciousness within him, and begins to steady himself upon a principle. The realization of unchanging principles in consciousness is at once the source and secret of the highest power.

When, after much searching, and suffering, and sacrificing, the light of an eternal principle dawns upon the soul, a divine calm ensues and joy unspeakable gladdens the heart.

He who has realized such a principle ceases to wander, and remains poised and self-possessed. He ceases to be "passion's slave," and becomes a master-builder in the Temple of Destiny.

The man that is governed by self, and not by a principle, changes his front when his selfish comforts are threatened. Deeply intent upon defending and guarding his own interests, he regards all means as lawful that will subserve that end. He is continually scheming as to how he may protect himself against his enemies, being too self-centered to perceive that he is his own enemy. Such a man's work crumbles away, for it is divorced from Truth and power. All effort that is grounded upon self, perishes; only that work endures that is built upon an indestructible principle.

The man that stands upon a principle is the same calm, dauntless, self-possessed man under all circumstances. When the hour of trial comes, and he has to decide between his personal comforts and Truth, he gives up his comforts and remains firm. Even the prospect of torture and death cannot alter or deter him. The man of self regards the loss of his wealth, his comforts, or his life as the greatest calamities which can befall him. The man of principle looks upon these incidents as comparatively insignificant, and not to be weighed with loss of character, loss of Truth. To desert Truth is, to him, the only happening which can really be called a calamity.

It is the hour of crisis which decides who are the minions of darkness, and who the children of Light. It is the epoch of threatening disaster, ruin, and persecution which divides the sheep from the goats, and reveals to the reverential gaze of succeeding ages the men and women of power.

It is easy for a man, so long as he is left in the enjoyment of his possessions, to persuade himself that he believes in and adheres to the principles of Peace, Brotherhood, and Universal Love; but if, when his enjoyments are threatened, or he imagines they are threatened, he begins to clamor loudly for war, he shows that he believes in and stands upon, not Peace, Brotherhood, and Love, but strife, selfishness, and hatred.

He who does not desert his principles when threatened with the loss of every earthly thing, even to the loss of reputation and life, is the man of power; is the man whose every word and work endures; is the man whom the afterworld honors, reveres, and worships. Rather than desert that principle of Divine Love on which he rested, and in which all his trust was placed, Jesus endured the utmost extremity of agony and deprivation; and today the world prostrates itself at his pierced feet in rapt adoration.

There is no way to the acquirement of spiritual power except by that inward illumination and enlightenment which is the realization of spiritual principles; and those principles can only be realized by constant practice and application.

Take the principle of divine Love, and quietly and diligently meditate upon it with the object of arriving at a thorough understanding of it. Bring its searching light to bear upon all your habits, your actions, your speech and intercourse with others, your every secret thought and desire. As you persevere in this course, the divine Love will become more and more perfectly revealed to you, and your own shortcomings will stand out in more and more vivid contrast, spurring you on to renewed endeavor; and having once caught a glimpse of the incomparable majesty of that imperishable principle, you will never again rest in your weakness, your selfishness, your imperfection, but will pursue that Love until you have relinquished every discordant element, and have brought yourself into perfect harmony with it. And that state of inward harmony is spiritual power. Take also other spiritual principles, such as Purity and Compassion, and apply them in the same way, and, so exacting is Truth, you will be able to make no stay, no resting-place until the inmost garment of your soul is bereft of every stain, and your heart has become incapable of any hard, condemnatory, and pitiless impulse.

Only in so far as you understand, realize, and rely upon, these principles, will you acquire spiritual power, and that power will be manifested in and through you in the form of increasing dispassion, patience and equanimity.

Dispassion argues superior self-control; sublime patience is the very hall-mark of divine knowledge, and to retain an unbroken calm amid all the duties and distractions of life, marks off the man of power. "It is easy in the world to live after the world's opinion; it is easy in solitude to live after our own; but the great man is he who in the midst of the crowd keeps with perfect sweetness the independence of solitude."

Some mystics hold that perfection in dispassion is the source of that power by which miracles (so-called) are performed, and truly he who has gained such perfect control of all his interior forces that no shock, however great, can for one moment unbalance him, must be capable of guiding and directing those forces with a master-hand.

To grow in self-control, in patience, in equanimity, is to grow in strength and power; and you can only thus grow by focusing your consciousness upon a principle. As a child, after making many and vigorous attempts to walk unaided, at last succeeds, after numerous falls, in accomplishing this, so you must enter the way of power by first attempting to stand alone. Break away from the tyranny of custom, tradition, conventionality, and the opinions of others, until you succeed in walking lonely and erect among men. Rely upon your own judgment; be true to your own conscience; follow the Light that is within you; all outward lights are so many will-o'-the-wisps. There will be those who will tell you that you are foolish; that your judgment is faulty; that your conscience is all awry, and that the Light within you is darkness; but heed them not. If what they say is true the sooner you, as a searcher for wisdom, find it out the better, and you can only make the discovery by bringing your powers to the test. Therefore, pursue your course bravely. Your conscience is at least your own, and to follow it is to be a man; to follow the conscience of another is to be a slave. You will have many falls, will suffer many wounds, will endure many buffetings for a time, but press on in faith, believing that sure and certain victory lies ahead. Search for a rock, a principle, and having found it cling to it; get it under your feet and stand erect upon it, until at last, immovably fixed upon it, you succeed in defying the fury of the waves and storms of selfishness.

For selfishness in any and every form is dissipation, weakness, death; unselfishness in its spiritual aspect is conservation, power, life. As you grow in spiritual life, and become established upon principles, you will become as beautiful and as unchangeable as those principles, will taste of the sweetness of their immortal essence, and will realize the eternal and indestructible nature of the God within.

> No harmful shaft can reach the righteous man,
> Standing erect amid the storms of hate,
> Defying hurt and injury and ban,
> Surrounded by the trembling slaves of Fate.
>
> Majestic in the strength of silent power,
> Serene he stands, nor changes not nor turns;
> Patient and firm in suffering's darkest hour,
> Time bends to him, and death and doom he spurns.
>
> Wrath's lurid lightnings round about him play,
> And hell's deep thunders roll about his head;
> Yet heeds he not, for him they cannot slay
> Who stands whence earth and time and space are fled.
>
> Sheltered by deathless love, what fear hath he?
> Armored in changeless Truth, what can he know
> Of loss and gain? Knowing eternity,
> He moves not whilst the shadows come and go.
>
> Call him immortal, call him Truth and Light
> And splendor of prophetic majesty
> Who bideth thus amid the powers of night,

Clothed with the glory of divinity.

The Realization of Selfless Love

It is said that Michael Angelo saw in every rough block of stone a thing of beauty awaiting the master-hand to bring it into reality. Even so, within each there reposes the Divine Image awaiting the master-hand of Faith and the chisel of Patience to bring it into manifestation. And that Divine Image is revealed and realized as stainless, selfless Love.

Hidden deep in every human heart, though frequently covered up with a mass of hard and almost impenetrable accretions, is the spirit of Divine Love, whose holy and spotless essence is undying and eternal. It is the Truth in man; it is that which belongs to the Supreme: that which is real and immortal. All else changes and passes away; this alone is permanent and imperishable; and to realize this Love by ceaseless diligence in the practice of the highest righteousness, to live in it and to become fully conscious in it, is to enter into immortality here and now, is to become one with Truth, one with God, one with the central Heart of all things, and to know our own divine and eternal nature.

To reach this Love, to understand and experience it, one must work with great persistency and diligence upon his heart and mind, must ever renew his patience and keep strong his faith, for there will be much to remove, much to accomplish before the Divine Image is revealed in all its glorious beauty.

He who strives to reach and to accomplish the divine will be tried to the very uttermost; and this is absolutely necessary, for how else could one acquire that sublime patience without which there is no real wisdom, no divinity? Ever and anon, as he proceeds, all his work will seem to be futile, and his efforts appear to be thrown away. Now and then a hasty touch will mar his image, and perhaps when he imagines his work is almost completed he will find what he imagined to be the beautiful form of Divine Love utterly destroyed, and he must begin again with his past bitter experience to guide and help him. But he who has resolutely set himself to realize the Highest recognizes no such thing as defeat. All failures are apparent, not real. Every slip, every fall, every return to selfishness is a lesson learned, an experience gained, from which a golden grain of wisdom is extracted, helping the striver toward the accomplishment of his lofty object. To recognize

"That of our vices we can frame
A ladder if we will but tread

Beneath our feet each deed of shame,"

is to enter the way that leads unmistakably toward the Divine, and the failings of one who thus recognizes are so many dead selves, upon which he rises, as upon stepping-stones, to higher things.

Once come to regard your failings, your sorrows and sufferings as so many voices telling you plainly where you are weak and faulty, where you fall below the true and the divine, you will then begin to ceaselessly watch yourself, and every slip, every pang of pain will show you where you are to set to work, and what you have to remove out of your heart in order to bring it nearer to the likeness of the Divine, nearer to the Perfect Love. And as you proceed, day by day detaching yourself more and more from the inward selfishness the Love that is selfless will gradually become revealed to you. And when you are growing patient and calm, when your petulances, tempers, and irritabilities are passing away from you, and the more powerful lusts and prejudices cease to dominate and enslave you, then you will know that the divine is awakening within you, that you are drawing near to the eternal Heart, that you are not far from that selfless Love, the possession of which is peace and immortality.

Divine Love is distinguished from human loves in this supremely important particular, it is free from partiality. Human loves cling to a particular object to the exclusion of all else, and when that object is removed, great and deep is the resultant suffering to the one who loves. Divine Love embraces the whole universe, and, without clinging to any part, yet contains within itself the whole, and he who comes to it by gradually purifying and broadening his human loves until all the selfish and impure elements are burnt out of them, ceases from suffering. It is because human loves are narrow and confined and mingled with selfishness that they cause suffering. No suffering can result from that Love which is so absolutely pure that it seeks nothing for itself. Nevertheless, human loves are absolutely necessary as steps toward the Divine, and no soul is prepared to partake of Divine Love until it has become capable of the deepest and most intense human love. It is only by passing through human loves and human sufferings that Divine Love is reached and realized.

All human loves are perishable like the forms to which they cling; but there is a Love that is imperishable, and that does not cling to appearances.

All human loves are counterbalanced by human hates; but there is a Love that admits of no opposite or reaction; divine and free from all taint of self, that sheds its fragrance on all alike.

Human loves are reflections of the Divine Love, and draw the soul nearer to the reality, the Love that knows neither sorrow nor change.

It is well that the mother, clinging with passionate tenderness to the little helpless form of flesh that lies on her bosom, should be overwhelmed with the dark waters of sorrow when she sees it laid in the cold earth. It is well that her tears should flow and her heart ache, for only thus can she be reminded of the evanescent nature of the joys and objects of sense, and be drawn nearer to the eternal and imperishable Reality.

It is well that lover, brother, sister, husband, wife should suffer deep anguish, and be enveloped in gloom when the visible object of their affections is torn from them, so that they may learn to turn their affections toward the invisible Source of all, where alone abiding satisfaction is to be found.

It is well that the proud, the ambitious, the self-seeking, should suffer defeat, humiliation, and misfortune; that they should pass through the scorching fires of affliction; for only thus can the wayward soul be brought to reflect upon the enigma of life; only thus can the heart be softened and purified, and prepared to receive the Truth.

When the sting of anguish penetrates the heart of human love; when gloom and loneliness and desertion cloud the soul of friendship and trust, then it is that the heart turns toward the sheltering love of the Eternal, and finds rest in its silent peace. And whosoever comes to this Love is not turned away comfortless, is not pierced with anguish nor surrounded with gloom; and is never deserted in the dark hour of trial.

The glory of Divine Love can only be revealed in the heart that is chastened by sorrow, and the image of the heavenly state can only be perceived and realized when the lifeless, formless accretions of ignorance and self are hewn away.

Only that Love that seeks no personal gratification or reward, that does not make distinctions, and that leaves behind no heartaches, can be called divine.

Men, clinging to self and to the comfortless shadows of evil, are in the habit of thinking of divine Love as something belonging to a God who is out of reach; as something outside themselves, and that must for ever remain outside. Truly, the Love of God is ever beyond the reach of self, but when the heart and mind are emptied of self then the selfless Love, the supreme Love, the Love that is of God or Good becomes an inward and abiding reality.

And this inward realization of holy Love is none other than the Love of Christ that is so much talked about and so little comprehended. The Love that not only saves the soul from sin, but lifts it also above the power of temptation.

But how may one attain to this sublime realization? The answer which Truth has always given, and will ever give to this question is,—"Empty thyself, and I will fill thee." Divine Love cannot be known until self is dead, for self is the denial of Love, and how can that which is known be also denied? Not until the stone of self is rolled away from the sepulcher of the soul does the immortal Christ, the pure Spirit of Love, hitherto crucified, dead and buried, cast off the bands of ignorance, and come forth in all the majesty of His resurrection.

You believe that the Christ of Nazareth was put to death and rose again. I do not say you err in that belief; but if you refuse to believe that the gentle spirit of Love is crucified daily upon the dark cross of your selfish desires, then, I say, you err in this unbelief, and have not yet perceived, even afar off, the Love of Christ.

You say that you have tasted of salvation in the Love of Christ. Are you saved from your temper, your irritability, your vanity, your personal dislikes, your judgment and condemnation of others? If not, from what are you saved, and wherein have you realized the transforming Love of Christ?

He who has realized the Love that is divine has become a new man, and has ceased to be swayed and dominated by the old elements of self. He is known for his patience, his purity, his self-control, his deep charity of heart, and his unalterable sweetness.

Divine or selfless Love is not a mere sentiment or emotion; it is a state of knowledge which destroys the dominion of evil and the belief in evil, and lifts the soul into the joyful realization of the supreme Good. To the divinely wise, knowledge and Love are one and inseparable.

It is toward the complete realization of this divine Love that the whole world is moving; it was for this purpose that the universe came into existence, and every grasping at happiness, every reaching out of the soul toward objects, ideas and ideals, is an effort to realize it. But the world does not realize this Love at present because it is grasping at the fleeting shadow and ignoring, in its blindness, the substance. And so suffering and sorrow continue, and must continue until the world, taught by its self-inflicted pains, discovers the Love that is selfless, the wisdom that is calm and full of peace.

And this Love, this Wisdom, this Peace, this tranquil state of mind and heart may be attained to, may be realized by all who are willing and ready to yield up self, and who are prepared to humbly enter into a comprehension of all that the giving up of self involves. There is no arbitrary power in the universe, and the strongest chains of fate by which men are bound are self-forged. Men are chained to that which causes suffering because they desire to be so, because they love their chains, because they think their little dark prison of self is sweet and beautiful, and they are afraid that if they desert that prison they will lose all that is real and worth having.

"Ye suffer from yourselves, none else compels,
None other holds ye that ye live and die."

And the indwelling power which forged the chains and built around itself the dark and narrow prison, can break away when it desires and wills to do so, and the soul does will to do so when it has discovered the worthlessness of its prison, when long suffering has prepared it for the reception of the boundless Light and Love.

As the shadow follows the form, and as smoke comes after fire, so effect follows cause, and suffering and bliss follow the thoughts and deeds of men. There is no effect in the world around us but has its hidden or revealed cause, and that cause is in accordance with absolute justice. Men reap a harvest of suffering because in the near or distant past they have sown the seeds of evil; they reap a harvest of bliss also as a result of their own sowing of the seeds of good. Let a man meditate upon this, let him strive to understand it, and he will then begin to sow only seeds of good, and will burn up the tares and weeds which he has formerly grown in the garden of his heart.

The world does not understand the Love that is selfless because it is engrossed in the pursuit of its own pleasures, and cramped within the narrow limits of perishable interests mistaking, in its ignorance, those pleasures and interests for real and abiding things. Caught in the flames of fleshly lusts, and burning with anguish, it sees not the pure and peaceful beauty of Truth. Feeding upon the swinish husks of error and self-delusion, it is shut out from the mansion of all-seeing Love.

Not having this Love, not understanding it, men institute innumerable reforms which involve no inward sacrifice, and each imagines that his reform is going to right the world for ever, while he himself continues to propagate evil by engaging it in his own heart. That only can be called reform which tends to reform the human heart, for all evil has its rise there, and not until the world, ceasing from selfishness and party strife, has learned the lesson of divine Love, will it realize the Golden Age of universal blessedness.

Let the rich cease to despise the poor, and the poor to condemn the rich; let the greedy learn how to give, and the lustful how to grow pure; let the partisan cease from strife, and the uncharitable begin to forgive; let the envious endeavor to rejoice with others, and the slanderers grow ashamed of their conduct. Let men and women take this course, and, lo! the Golden Age is at hand. He, therefore, who purifies his own heart is the world's greatest benefactor.

Yet, though the world is, and will be for many ages to come, shut out from that Age of Gold, which is the realization of selfless Love, you, if you are willing, may enter it now, by rising above your selfish self; if you will pass from prejudice, hatred, and condemnation, to gentle and forgiving love.

Where hatred, dislike, and condemnation are, selfless Love does not abide.
It resides only in the heart that has ceased from all condemnation.

You say, "How can I love the drunkard, the hypocrite, the sneak, the murderer? I am compelled to dislike and condemn such men." It is true you cannot love such men emotionally, but when you say that you must perforce dislike and condemn them you show that you are not acquainted with the Great over-ruling Love; for it is possible to attain to such a state of interior enlightenment as will enable you to perceive the train of causes by which these men have become as they are, to enter into their intense sufferings, and to know the certainty of their ultimate purification. Possessed of such knowledge it will be utterly impossible for you any longer to dislike or condemn them, and you will always think of them with perfect calmness and deep compassion.

If you love people and speak of them with praise until they in some way thwart you, or do something of which you disapprove, and then you dislike them and speak of them with dispraise, you are not governed by the Love which is of God. If, in your heart, you are continually arraigning and condemning others, selfless Love is hidden from you.

He who knows that Love is at the heart of all things, and has realized the all-sufficing power of that Love, has no room in his heart for condemnation.

Men, not knowing this Love, constitute themselves judge and executioner of their fellows, forgetting that there is the Eternal Judge and Executioner, and in so far as men deviate from them in their own views, their particular reforms and methods, they brand them as fanatical, unbalanced, lacking judgment, sincerity, and honesty; in so far as others approximate to their own standard do they look upon them as being everything that is admirable. Such are the men who are centered in self. But he whose heart is centered in the supreme Love does not so brand and classify men; does not seek to convert men to his own views, not to convince them of the superiority of his methods. Knowing the Law of Love, he lives it, and maintains the same calm attitude of mind and sweetness of heart toward all. The debased and the virtuous, the foolish and the wise, the learned and the unlearned, the selfish and the unselfish receive alike the benediction of his tranquil thought.

You can only attain to this supreme knowledge, this divine Love by unremitting endeavor in self-discipline, and by gaining victory after victory over yourself. Only the pure in heart see God, and when your heart is sufficiently purified you will enter into the New Birth, and the Love that does not die, nor change, nor end in pain and sorrow will be awakened within you, and you will be at peace.

He who strives for the attainment of divine Love is ever seeking to overcome the spirit of condemnation, for where there is pure spiritual knowledge, condemnation cannot exist, and only in the heart that has become incapable of condemnation is Love perfected and fully realized.

The Christian condemns the Atheist; the Atheist satirizes the Christian; the Catholic and Protestant are ceaselessly engaged in wordy warfare, and the spirit of strife and hatred rules where peace and love should be.

"He that hateth his brother is a murderer," a crucifier of the divine Spirit of Love; and until you can regard men of all religions and of no religion with the same impartial spirit, with all freedom from dislike, and with perfect equanimity, you have yet to strive for that Love which bestows upon its possessor freedom and salvation.

The realization of divine knowledge, selfless Love, utterly destroys the spirit of condemnation, disperses all evil, and lifts the consciousness to that height of pure vision where Love, Goodness, Justice are seen to be universal, supreme, all-conquering, indestructible.

Train your mind in strong, impartial, and gentle thought; train your heart in purity and compassion; train your tongue to silence and to true and stainless speech; so shall you enter the way of holiness and peace, and shall ultimately realize the immortal Love. So living, without seeking to convert, you will convince; without arguing, you will teach; not cherishing ambition, the wise will find you out; and without striving to gain men's opinions, you will subdue their hearts. For Love is all-conquering, all-powerful; and the thoughts, and deeds, and words of Love can never perish.

To know that Love is universal, supreme, all-sufficing; to be freed from the trammels of evil; to be quit of the inward unrest; to know that all men are striving to realize the Truth each in his own way; to be satisfied, sorrowless, serene; this is peace; this is gladness; this is immortality; this is Divinity; this is the realization of selfless Love.

> I stood upon the shore, and saw the rocks
> Resist the onslaught of the mighty sea,
> And when I thought how all the countless shocks
> They had withstood through an eternity,
> I said, "To wear away this solid main

The ceaseless efforts of the waves are vain."

But when I thought how they the rocks had rent,
And saw the sand and shingles at my feet
(Poor passive remnants of resistance spent)
Tumbled and tossed where they the waters meet,
Then saw I ancient landmarks 'neath the waves,
And knew the waters held the stones their slaves.

I saw the mighty work the waters wrought
By patient softness and unceasing flow;
How they the proudest promontory brought
Unto their feet, and massy hills laid low;
How the soft drops the adamantine wall
Conquered at last, and brought it to its fall.

And then I knew that hard, resisting sin
Should yield at last to Love's soft ceaseless roll
Coming and going, ever flowing in
Upon the proud rocks of the human soul;
That all resistance should be spent and past,
And every heart yield unto it at last.

Entering into the Infinite

From the beginning of time, man, in spite of his bodily appetites and desires, in the midst of all his clinging to earthly and impermanent things, has ever been intuitively conscious of the limited, transient, and illusionary nature of his material existence, and in his sane and silent moments has tried to reach out into a comprehension of the Infinite, and has turned with tearful aspiration toward the restful Reality of the Eternal Heart.

While vainly imagining that the pleasures of earth are real and satisfying, pain and sorrow continually remind him of their unreal and unsatisfying nature. Ever striving to believe that complete satisfaction is to be found in material things, he is conscious of an inward and persistent revolt against this belief, which revolt is at once a refutation of his essential mortality, and an inherent and imperishable proof that only in the immortal, the eternal, the infinite can he find abiding satisfaction and unbroken peace.

And here is the common ground of faith; here the root and spring of all religion; here the soul of Brotherhood and the heart of Love,—that man is essentially and spiritually divine and eternal, and that, immersed in mortality and troubled with unrest, he is ever striving to enter into a consciousness of his real nature.

The spirit of man is inseparable from the Infinite, and can be satisfied with nothing short of the Infinite, and the burden of pain will continue to weigh upon man's heart, and the shadows of sorrow to darken his pathway until, ceasing from his wanderings in the dream-world of matter, he comes back to his home in the reality of the Eternal.

As the smallest drop of water detached from the ocean contains all the qualities of the ocean, so man, detached in consciousness from the Infinite, contains within him its likeness; and as the drop of water must, by the law of its nature, ultimately find its way back to the ocean and lose itself in its silent depths, so must man, by the unfailing law of his nature, at last return to his source, and lose himself in the great ocean of the Infinite.

To re-become one with the Infinite is the goal of man. To enter into perfect harmony with the Eternal Law is Wisdom, Love and Peace. But this divine state is, and must ever be, incomprehensible to the merely personal. Personality, separateness, selfishness are one and the same, and are the antithesis of wisdom and divinity. By the unqualified surrender of the personality, separateness and selfishness cease, and man enters into the possession of his divine heritage of immortality and infinity.

Such surrender of the personality is regarded by the worldly and selfish mind as the most grievous of all calamities, the most irreparable loss, yet it is the one supreme and incomparable blessing, the only real and lasting gain. The mind unenlightened upon the inner laws of being, and upon the nature and destiny of its own life, clings to transient appearances, things which have in them no enduring substantiality, and so clinging, perishes, for the time being, amid the shattered wreckage of its own illusions.

Men cling to and gratify the flesh as though it were going to last for ever, and though they try to forget the nearness and inevitability of its dissolution, the dread of death and of the loss of all that they cling to clouds their happiest hours, and the chilling shadow of their own selfishness follows them like a remorseless specter.

And with the accumulation of temporal comforts and luxuries, the divinity within men is drugged, and they sink deeper and deeper into materiality, into the perishable life of the senses, and where there is sufficient intellect, theories concerning the immortality of the flesh come to be regarded as infallible truths. When a man's soul is clouded with selfishness in any or every form, he loses the power of spiritual discrimination, and confuses the temporal with the eternal, the perishable with the permanent, mortality with immortality, and error with Truth. It is thus that the world has come to be filled with theories and speculations having no foundation in human experience. Every body of flesh contains within itself, from the hour of birth, the elements of its own destruction, and by the unalterable law of its own nature must it pass away.

The perishable in the universe can never become permanent; the permanent can never pass away; the mortal can never become immortal; the immortal can never die; the temporal cannot become eternal nor the eternal become temporal; appearance can never become reality, nor reality fade into appearance; error can never become Truth, nor can Truth become error. Man cannot immortalize the flesh, but, by overcoming the flesh, by relinquishing all its inclinations, he can enter the region of immortality. "God alone hath immortality," and only by realizing the God state of consciousness does man enter into immortality.

All nature in its myriad forms of life is changeable, impermanent, unenduring. Only the informing Principle of nature endures. Nature is many, and is marked by separation. The informing Principle is One, and is marked by unity. By overcoming the senses and the selfishness within, which is the overcoming of nature, man emerges from the chrysalis of the personal and illusory, and wings himself into the glorious light of the impersonal, the region of universal Truth, out of which all perishable forms come.

Let men, therefore, practice self-denial; let them conquer their animal inclinations; let them refuse to be enslaved by luxury and pleasure; let them practice virtue, and grow daily into high and ever higher virtue, until at last they grow into the Divine, and enter into both the practice and the comprehension of humility, meekness, forgiveness, compassion, and love, which practice and comprehension constitute Divinity.

"Good-will gives insight," and only he who has so conquered his personality that he has but one attitude of mind, that of good-will, toward all creatures, is possessed of divine insight, and is capable of distinguishing the true from the false. The supremely good man is, therefore, the wise man, the divine man, the enlightened seer, the knower of the Eternal. Where you find unbroken gentleness, enduring patience, sublime lowliness, graciousness of speech, self-control, self-forgetfulness, and deep and abounding sympathy, look there for the highest wisdom, seek the company of such a one, for he has realized the Divine, he lives with the Eternal, he has become one with the Infinite. Believe not him that is impatient, given to anger, boastful, who clings to pleasure and refuses to renounce his selfish gratifications, and who practices not good-will and far-reaching compassion, for such a one hath not wisdom, vain is all his knowledge, and his works and words will perish, for they are grounded on that which passes away.

Let a man abandon self, let him overcome the world, let him deny the personal; by this pathway only can he enter into the heart of the Infinite.

The world, the body, the personality are mirages upon the desert of time; transitory dreams in the dark night of spiritual slumber, and those who have crossed the desert, those who are spiritually awakened, have alone comprehended the Universal Reality where all appearances are dispersed and dreaming and delusion are destroyed.

There is one Great Law which exacts unconditional obedience, one unifying principle which is the basis of all diversity, one eternal Truth wherein all the problems of earth pass away like shadows. To realize this Law, this Unity, this Truth, is to enter into the Infinite, is to become one with the Eternal.

To center one's life in the Great Law of Love is to enter into rest, harmony, peace. To refrain from all participation in evil and discord; to cease from all resistance to evil, and from the omission of that which is good, and to fall back upon unswerving obedience to the holy calm within, is to enter into the inmost heart of things, is to attain to a living, conscious experience of that eternal and infinite principle which must ever remain a hidden mystery to the merely perceptive intellect. Until this principle is realized, the soul is not established in peace, and he who so realizes is truly wise; not wise with the wisdom of the learned, but with the simplicity of a blameless heart and of a divine manhood.

To enter into a realization of the Infinite and Eternal is to rise superior to time, and the world, and the body, which comprise the kingdom of darkness; and is to become established in immortality, Heaven, and the Spirit, which make up the Empire of Light.

Entering into the Infinite is not a mere theory or sentiment. It is a vital experience which is the result of assiduous practice in inward purification. When the body is no longer believed to be, even remotely, the real man; when all appetites and desires are thoroughly subdued and purified; when the emotions are rested and calm, and when the oscillation of the intellect ceases and perfect poise is secured, then, and not till then, does consciousness become one with the Infinite; not until then is childlike wisdom and profound peace secured.

Men grow weary and gray over the dark problems of life, and finally pass away and leave them unsolved because they cannot see their way out of the darkness of the personality, being too much engrossed in its limitations. Seeking to save his personal life, man forfeits the greater impersonal Life in Truth; clinging to the perishable, he is shut out from a knowledge of the Eternal.

By the surrender of self all difficulties are overcome, and there is no error in the universe but the fire of inward sacrifice will burn it up like chaff; no problem, however great, but will disappear like a shadow under the searching light of self-abnegation. Problems exist only in our own self-created illusions, and they vanish away when self is yielded up. Self and error are synonymous. Error is involved in the darkness of unfathomable complexity, but eternal simplicity is the glory of Truth.

Love of self shuts men out from Truth, and seeking their own personal happiness they lose the deeper, purer, and more abiding bliss. Says Carlyle—"There is in man a higher than love of happiness. He can do without happiness, and instead thereof find blessedness.

... Love not pleasure, love God. This is the Everlasting Yea, wherein all contradiction is solved; wherein whoso walks and works, it is well with him."

He who has yielded up that self, that personality that men most love, and to which they cling with such fierce tenacity, has left behind him all perplexity, and has entered into a simplicity so profoundly simple as to be looked upon by the world, involved as it is in a network of error, as foolishness. Yet such a one has realized the highest wisdom, and is at rest in the Infinite. He "accomplishes without striving," and all problems melt before him, for he has entered the region of reality, and deals, not with changing effects, but with the unchanging principles of things. He is enlightened with a wisdom which is as superior to ratiocination, as reason is to animality. Having yielded up his lusts, his errors, his opinions and prejudices, he has entered into possession of the knowledge of God, having slain the selfish desire for heaven, and along with it the ignorant fear of hell; having relinquished even the love of life itself, he has gained supreme bliss and Life Eternal, the Life which bridges life and death, and knows its own immortality. Having yielded up all without reservation, he has gained all, and rests in peace on the bosom of the Infinite.

Only he who has become so free from self as to be equally content to be annihilated as to live, or to live as to be annihilated, is fit to enter into the Infinite. Only he who, ceasing to trust his perishable self, has learned to trust in boundless measure the Great Law, the Supreme Good, is prepared to partake of undying bliss.

For such a one there is no more regret, nor disappointment, nor remorse, for where all selfishness has ceased these sufferings cannot be; and whatever happens to him he knows that it is for his own good, and he is content, being no longer the servant of self, but the servant of the Supreme. He is no longer affected by the changes of earth, and when he hears of wars and rumors of wars his peace is not disturbed, and where men grow angry and cynical and quarrelsome, he bestows compassion and love. Though appearances may contradict it, he knows that the world is progressing, and that

> "Through its laughing and its weeping,
> Through its living and its keeping,
> Through its follies and its labors, weaving in and out of sight,
> To the end from the beginning,
> Through all virtue and all sinning,
> Reeled from God's great spool of Progress, runs the golden
> thread of light."

When a fierce storm is raging none are angered about it, because they know it will quickly pass away, and when the storms of contention are devastating the world, the wise man, looking with the eye of Truth and pity, knows that it will pass away, and that out of the wreckage of broken hearts which it leaves behind the immortal Temple of Wisdom will be built.

Sublimely patient; infinitely compassionate; deep, silent, and pure, his very presence is a benediction; and when he speaks men ponder his words in their hearts, and by them rise to higher levels of attainment. Such is he who has entered into the Infinite, who by the power of utmost sacrifice has solved the sacred mystery of life.

> Questioning Life and Destiny and Truth,
> I sought the dark and labyrinthine Sphinx,
> Who spake to me this strange and wondrous thing:—
> "Concealment only lies in blinded eyes,
> And God alone can see the Form of God."
>
> I sought to solve this hidden mystery
> Vainly by paths of blindness and of pain,
> But when I found the Way of Love and Peace,
> Concealment ceased, and I was blind no more:
> Then saw I God e'en with the eyes of God.

Saints, Sages and Saviors: The Law of Service

The spirit of Love which is manifested as a perfect and rounded life, is the crown of being and the supreme end of knowledge upon this earth.

The measure of a man's truth is the measure of his love, and Truth is far removed from him whose life is not governed by Love. The intolerant and condemnatory, even though they profess the highest religion, have the smallest measure of Truth; while those who exercise patience, and who listen calmly and dispassionately to all sides, and both arrive themselves at, and incline others to, thoughtful and unbiased conclusions upon all problems and issues, have Truth in fullest measure. The final test of wisdom is this,— how does a man live? What spirit does he manifest? How does he act under trial and temptation? Many men boast of being in possession of Truth who are continually swayed by grief, disappointment, and passion, and who sink under the first little trial that comes along. Truth is nothing if not unchangeable, and in so far as a man takes his stand upon Truth does he become steadfast in virtue, does he rise superior to his passions and emotions and changeable personality.

Men formulate perishable dogmas, and call them Truth. Truth cannot be formulated; it is ineffable, and ever beyond the reach of intellect. It can only be experienced by practice; it can only be manifested as a stainless heart and a perfect life.

Who, then, in the midst of the ceaseless pandemonium of schools and creeds and parties, has the Truth? He who lives it. He who practices it. He who, having risen above that pandemonium by overcoming himself, no longer engages in it, but sits apart, quiet, subdued, calm, and self-possessed, freed from all strife, all bias, all condemnation, and bestows upon all the glad and unselfish love of the divinity within him.

He who is patient, calm, gentle, and forgiving under all circumstances, manifests the Truth. Truth will never be proved by wordy arguments and learned treatises, for if men do not perceive the Truth in infinite patience, undying forgiveness, and all-embracing compassion, no words can ever prove it to them.

It is an easy matter for the passionate to be calm and patient when they are alone, or are in the midst of calmness. It is equally easy for the uncharitable to be gentle and kind when they are dealt kindly with, but he who retains his patience and calmness under all trial, who remains sublimely meek and gentle under the most trying circumstances, he, and he alone, is possessed of the spotless Truth. And this is so because such lofty virtues belong to the Divine, and can only be manifested by one who has attained to the highest wisdom, who has relinquished his passionate and self-seeking nature, who has realized the supreme and unchangeable Law, and has brought himself into harmony with it.

Let men, therefore, cease from vain and passionate arguments about Truth, and let them think and say and do those things which make for harmony, peace, love, and good-will. Let them practice heart-virtue, and search humbly and diligently for the Truth which frees the soul from all error and sin, from all that blights the human heart, and that darkens, as with unending night, the pathway of the wandering souls of earth.

There is one great all-embracing Law which is the foundation and cause of the universe, the Law of Love. It has been called by many names in various countries and at various times, but behind all its names the same unalterable Law may be discovered by the eye of Truth. Names, religions, personalities pass away, but the Law of Love remains. To become possessed of a knowledge of this Law, to enter into conscious harmony with it, is to become immortal, invincible, indestructible.

It is because of the effort of the soul to realize this Law that men come again and again to live, to suffer, and to die; and when realized, suffering ceases, personality is dispersed, and the fleshly life and death are destroyed, for consciousness becomes one with the Eternal.

The Law is absolutely impersonal, and its highest manifested expression is that of Service. When the purified heart has realized Truth it is then called upon to make the last, the greatest and holiest sacrifice, the sacrifice of the well-earned enjoyment of Truth. It is by virtue of this sacrifice that the divinely-emancipated soul comes to dwell among men, clothed with a body of flesh, content to dwell among the lowliest and least, and to be esteemed the servant of all mankind. That sublime humility which is manifested by the world's saviors is the seal of Godhead, and he who has annihilated the personality, and has become a living, visible manifestation of the impersonal, eternal, boundless Spirit of Love, is alone singled out as worthy to receive the unstinted worship of posterity. He only who succeeds in humbling himself with that divine humility which is not only the extinction of self, but is also the pouring out upon all the spirit of unselfish love, is exalted above measure, and given spiritual dominion in the hearts of mankind.

All the great spiritual teachers have denied themselves personal luxuries, comforts, and rewards, have abjured temporal power, and have lived and taught the limitless and impersonal Truth. Compare their lives and teachings, and you will find the same simplicity, the same self-sacrifice, the same humility, love, and peace both lived and preached by them. They taught the same eternal Principles, the realization of which destroys all evil. Those who have been hailed and worshiped as the saviors of mankind are manifestations of the Great impersonal Law, and being such, were free from passion and prejudice, and having no opinions, and no special letter of doctrine to preach and defend, they never sought to convert and to proselytize. Living in the highest Goodness, the supreme Perfection, their sole object was to uplift mankind by manifesting that Goodness in thought, word, and deed. They stand between man the personal and God the impersonal, and serve as exemplary types for the salvation of self-enslaved mankind.

Men who are immersed in self, and who cannot comprehend the Goodness that is absolutely impersonal, deny divinity to all saviors except their own, and thus introduce personal hatred and doctrinal controversy, and, while defending their own particular views with passion, look upon each other as being heathens or infidels, and so render null and void, as far as their lives are concerned, the unselfish beauty and holy grandeur of the lives and teachings of their own Masters. Truth cannot be limited; it can never be the special prerogative of any man, school, or nation, and when personality steps in, Truth is lost.

The glory alike of the saint, the sage, and the savior is this,—that he has realized the most profound lowliness, the most sublime unselfishness; having given up all, even his own personality, all his works are holy and enduring, for they are freed from every taint of self. He gives, yet never thinks of receiving; he works without regretting the past or anticipating the future, and never looks for reward.

When the farmer has tilled and dressed his land and put in the seed, he knows that he has done all that he can possibly do, and that now he must trust to the elements, and wait patiently for the course of time to bring about the harvest, and that no amount of expectancy on his part will affect the result. Even so, he who has realized Truth goes forth as a sower of the seeds of goodness, purity, love and peace, without expectancy, and never looking for results, knowing that there is the Great Over-ruling Law which brings about its own harvest in due time, and which is alike the source of preservation and destruction.

Men, not understanding the divine simplicity of a profoundly unselfish heart, look upon their particular savior as the manifestation of a special miracle, as being something entirely apart and distinct from the nature of things, and as being, in his ethical excellence, eternally unapproachable by the whole of mankind. This attitude of unbelief (for such it is) in the divine perfectibility of man, paralyzes effort, and binds the souls of men as with strong ropes to sin and suffering. Jesus "grew in wisdom" and was "perfected by suffering." What Jesus was, he became such; what Buddha was, he became such; and every holy man became such by unremitting perseverance in self-sacrifice. Once recognize this, once realize that by watchful effort and hopeful perseverance you can rise above your lower nature, and great and glorious will be the vistas of attainment that will open out before you. Buddha vowed that he would not relax his efforts until he arrived at the state of perfection, and he accomplished his purpose.

What the saints, sages, and saviors have accomplished, you likewise may accomplish if you will only tread the way which they trod and pointed out, the way of self-sacrifice, of self-denying service.

Truth is very simple. It says, "Give up self," "Come unto Me" (away from all that defiles) "and I will give you rest." All the mountains of commentary that have been piled upon it cannot hide it from the heart that is earnestly seeking for Righteousness. It does not require learning; it can be known in spite of learning. Disguised under many forms by erring self-seeking man, the beautiful simplicity and clear transparency of Truth remains unaltered and undimmed, and the unselfish heart enters into and partakes of its shining radiance. Not by weaving complex theories, not by building up speculative philosophies is Truth realized; but by weaving the web of inward purity, by building up the Temple of a stainless life is Truth realized.

He who enters upon this holy way begins by restraining his passions. This is virtue, and is the beginning of saintship, and saintship is the beginning of holiness. The entirely worldly man gratifies all his desires, and practices no more restraint than the law of the land in which he lives demands; the virtuous man restrains his passions; the saint attacks the enemy of Truth in its stronghold within his own heart, and restrains all selfish and impure thoughts; while the holy man is he who is free from passion and all impure thought, and to whom goodness and purity have become as natural as scent and color are to the flower. The holy man is divinely wise; he alone knows Truth in its fullness, and has entered into abiding rest and peace. For him evil has ceased; it has disappeared in the universal light of the All-Good. Holiness is the badge of wisdom. Said Krishna to the Prince Arjuna—

> "Humbleness, truthfulness, and harmlessness,
> Patience and honor, reverence for the wise,
> Purity, constancy, control of self,
> Contempt of sense-delights, self-sacrifice,
> Perception of the certitude of ill
> In birth, death, age, disease, suffering and sin;
> An ever tranquil heart in fortunes good
> And fortunes evil, ...
> ... Endeavors resolute
> To reach perception of the utmost soul,
> And grace to understand what gain it were
> So to attain—this is true wisdom, Prince!
> And what is otherwise is ignorance!"

Whoever fights ceaselessly against his own selfishness, and strives to supplant it with all-embracing love, is a saint, whether he live in a cottage or in the midst of riches and influence; or whether he preaches or remains obscure.

To the worldling, who is beginning to aspire towards higher things, the saint, such as a sweet St. Francis of Assisi, or a conquering St. Anthony, is a glorious and inspiring spectacle; to the saint, an equally enrapturing sight is that of the sage, sitting serene and holy, the conqueror of sin and sorrow, no more tormented by regret and remorse, and whom even temptation can never reach; and yet even the sage is drawn on by a still more glorious vision, that of the savior actively manifesting his knowledge in selfless works, and rendering his divinity more potent for good by sinking himself in the throbbing, sorrowing, aspiring heart of mankind.

And this only is true service—to forget oneself in love towards all, to lose oneself in working for the whole. O thou vain and foolish man, who thinkest that thy many works can save thee; who, chained to all error, talkest loudly of thyself, thy work, and thy many sacrifices, and magnifiest thine own importance; know this, that though thy fame fill the whole earth, all thy work shall come to dust, and thou thyself be reckoned lower than the least in the Kingdom of Truth!

Only the work that is impersonal can live; the works of self are both powerless and perishable. Where duties, howsoever humble, are done without self-interest, and with joyful sacrifice, there is true service and enduring work. Where deeds, however brilliant and apparently successful, are done from love of self, there is ignorance of the Law of Service, and the work perishes.

It is given to the world to learn one great and divine lesson, the lesson of absolute unselfishness. The saints, sages, and saviors of all time are they who have submitted themselves to this task, and have learned and lived it. All the Scriptures of the world are framed to teach this one lesson; all the great teachers reiterate it. It is too simple for the world which, scorning it, stumbles along in the complex ways of selfishness.

A pure heart is the end of all religion and the beginning of divinity. To search for this Righteousness is to walk the Way of Truth and Peace, and he who enters this Way will soon perceive that Immortality which is independent of birth and death, and will realize that in the Divine economy of the universe the humblest effort is not lost.

The divinity of a Krishna, a Gautama, or a Jesus is the crowning glory of self-abnegation, the end of the soul's pilgrimage in matter and mortality, and the world will not have finished its long journey until every soul has become as these, and has entered into the blissful realization of its own divinity.

> Great glory crowns the heights of hope by arduous struggle won;
> Bright honor rounds the hoary head that mighty works hath done;
> Fair riches come to him who strives in ways of golden gain.
> And fame enshrines his name who works with genius-glowing brain;
> But greater glory waits for him who, in the bloodless strife
> 'Gainst self and wrong, adopts, in love, the sacrificial life;
> And brighter honor rounds the brow of him who, 'mid the scorns
> Of blind idolaters of self, accepts the crown of thorns;
> And fairer purer riches come to him who greatly strives
> To walk in ways of love and truth to sweeten human lives;
> And he who serveth well mankind exchanges fleeting fame
> For Light eternal, Joy and Peace, and robes of heavenly flame.

The Realization of Perfect Pace

In the external universe there is ceaseless turmoil, change, and unrest; at the heart of all things there is undisturbed repose; in this deep silence dwelleth the Eternal.

Man partakes of this duality, and both the surface change and disquietude, and the deep-seated eternal abode of Peace, are contained within him.

As there are silent depths in the ocean which the fiercest storm cannot reach, so there are silent, holy depths in the heart of man which the storms of sin and sorrow can never disturb. To reach this silence and to live consciously in it is peace.

Discord is rife in the outward world, but unbroken harmony holds sway at the heart of the universe. The human soul, torn by discordant passion and grief, reaches blindly toward the harmony of the sinless state, and to reach this state and to live consciously in it is peace.

Hatred severs human lives, fosters persecution, and hurls nations into ruthless war, yet men, though they do not understand why, retain some measure of faith in the overshadowing of a Perfect Love; and to reach this Love and to live consciously in it is peace.

And this inward peace, this silence, this harmony, this Love, is the Kingdom of Heaven, which is so difficult to reach because few are willing to give up themselves and to become as little children.

> "Heaven's gate is very narrow and minute,

It cannot be perceived by foolish men
Blinded by vain illusions of the world;
E'en the clear-sighted who discern the way,
And seek to enter, find the portal barred,
And hard to be unlocked. Its massive bolts
Are pride and passion, avarice and lust."

Men cry peace! peace! where there is no peace, but on the contrary, discord, disquietude and strife. Apart from that Wisdom which is inseparable from self-renunciation, there can be no real and abiding peace.

The peace which results from social comfort, passing gratification, or worldly victory is transitory in its nature, and is burnt up in the heat of fiery trial. Only the Peace of Heaven endures through all trial, and only the selfless heart can know the Peace of Heaven.

Holiness alone is undying peace. Self-control leads to it, and the ever-increasing Light of Wisdom guides the pilgrim on his way. It is partaken of in a measure as soon as the path of virtue is entered upon, but it is only realized in its fullness when self disappears in the consummation of a stainless life.

"This is peace,
To conquer love of self and lust of life,
To tear deep-rooted passion from the heart
To still the inward strife."

If, O reader! you would realize the Light that never fades, the Joy that never ends, and the tranquillity that cannot be disturbed; if you would leave behind for ever your sins, your sorrows, your anxieties and perplexities; if, I say, you would partake of this salvation, this supremely glorious Life, then conquer yourself. Bring every thought, every impulse, every desire into perfect obedience to the divine power resident within you. There is no other way to peace but this, and if you refuse to walk it, your much praying and your strict adherence to ritual will be fruitless and unavailing, and neither gods nor angels can help you. Only to him that overcometh is given the white stone of the regenerate life, on which is written the New and Ineffable Name.

Come away, for awhile, from external things, from the pleasures of the senses, from the arguments of the intellect, from the noise and the excitements of the world, and withdraw yourself into the inmost chamber of your heart, and there, free from the sacrilegious intrusion of all selfish desires, you will find a deep silence, a holy calm, a blissful repose, and if you will rest awhile in that holy place, and will meditate there, the faultless eye of Truth will open within you, and you will see things as they really are. This holy place within you is your real and eternal self; it is the divine within you; and only when you identify yourself with it can you be said to be "clothed and in your right mind." It is the abode of peace, the temple of wisdom, the dwelling-place of immortality. Apart from this inward resting-place, this Mount of Vision, there can be no true peace, no knowledge of the Divine, and if you can remain there for one minute, one hour, or one day, it is possible for you to remain there always. All your sins and sorrows, your fears and anxieties are your own, and you can cling to them or you can give them up. Of your own accord you cling to your unrest; of your own accord you can come to abiding peace. No one else can give up sin for you; you must give it up yourself. The greatest teacher can do no more than walk the way of Truth for himself, and point it out to you; you yourself must walk it for yourself. You can obtain freedom and peace alone by your own efforts, by yielding up that which binds the soul, and which is destructive of peace.

The angels of divine peace and joy are always at hand, and if you do not see them, and hear them, and dwell with them, it is because you shut yourself out from them, and prefer the company of the spirits of evil within you. You are what you will to be, what you wish to be, what you prefer to be. You can commence to purify yourself, and by so doing can arrive at peace, or you can refuse to purify yourself, and so remain with suffering.

Step aside, then; come out of the fret and the fever of life; away from the scorching heat of self, and enter the inward resting-place where the cooling airs of peace will calm, renew, and restore you.

Come out of the storms of sin and anguish. Why be troubled and tempest-tossed when the haven of Peace of God is yours!

Give up all self-seeking; give up self, and lo! the Peace of God is yours!

Subdue the animal within you; conquer every selfish uprising, every discordant voice; transmute the base metals of your selfish nature into the unalloyed gold of Love, and you shall realize the Life of Perfect Peace. Thus subduing, thus conquering, thus transmuting, you will, O reader! while living in the flesh, cross the dark waters of mortality, and will reach that Shore upon which the storms of sorrow never beat, and where sin and suffering and dark uncertainty cannot come. Standing upon that Shore, holy, compassionate, awakened, and self-possessed and glad with unending gladness, you will realize that

"Never the Spirit was born, the Spirit will cease to be never;
Never was time it was not, end and beginning are dreams;

Birthless and deathless and changeless remaineth the Spirit for ever;
Death hath not touched it at all, dead though the house of it seems."

You will then know the meaning of Sin, of Sorrow, of Suffering, and that the end thereof is Wisdom; will know the cause and the issue of existence.

And with this realization you will enter into rest, for this is the bliss of immortality, this the unchangeable gladness, this the untrammeled knowledge, undefiled Wisdom, and undying Love; this, and this only, is the realization of Perfect Peace.

O thou who wouldst teach men of Truth!
Hast thou passed through the desert of doubt?
Art thou purged by the fires of sorrow? hath ruth
The fiends of opinion cast out
Of thy human heart? Is thy soul so fair
That no false thought can ever harbor there?

O thou who wouldst teach men of Love!
Hast thou passed through the place of despair?
Hast thou wept through the dark night of grief?
does it move
(Now freed from its sorrow and care)
Thy human heart to pitying gentleness,
Looking on wrong, and hate, and ceaseless stress?

O thou who wouldst teach men of Peace!
Hast thou crossed the wide ocean of strife?
Hast thou found on the Shores of the Silence,
Release from all the wild unrest of life?
From thy human heart hath all striving gone,
Leaving but Truth, and Love, and Peace alone?

THE END

The Heavenly Life

1. The Divine Centre

THE secret of life, of abundant life, with its strength, its felicity, and its unbroken peace is to find the Divine Centre within oneself, and to live in and from that, instead of in that outer circumference of disturbances — the clamours, cravings, and argumentations which make up the animal and intellectual man. These selfish elements constitute the mere husks of life, and must be thrown away by him who would penetrate to the Central Heart of things — to Life itself.

Not to know that within you that is changeless, and defiant of time and death, is not to know anything, but is to play vainly with the unsubstantial reflections in the Mirror of Time. Not to find within you those passionless Principles which are not moved by the strifes and shows and vanities of the world, is to find nothing but illusions which vanish as they are grasped.

He who resolves that he will not rest satisfied with appearances, shadows, illusions shall, by the piercing light of that resolve, disperse every fleeting phantasy, and shall enter into the substance and reality of life. He shall learn how to live, and he shall live. He shall be the slave of no passion, the servant of no opinion, the votary of no fond error. Finding the Divine Centre within his own heart, he will be pure and calm and strong and wise, and will ceaselessly radiate the Heavenly Life in which he lives — which is himself.

Having betaken himself to the Divine Refuge within, and remaining there, a man is free from sin. All his yesterdays are as the tide-washed and untrodden sands; no sin shall rise up against him to torment and accuse him and destroy his sacred peace; the fires of remorse cannot scorch him, nor can the storms of regret devastate his dwelling-place. His to-morrows are as seeds which shall germinate, bursting into beauty and potency of life, and no doubt shall shake his trust, no uncertainty rob him of repose. The Present is his, only in the immortal Present does he live, and it is as the eternal vault of blue above which looks down silently and calmly, yet radiant with purity and light, upon the upturned and tear-stained faces of the centuries.

Men love their desires, for gratification seems sweet to them, but its end is pain and vacuity; they love the argumentations of the intellect, for egotism seems most desirable to them, but the fruits thereof are humiliation and sorrow. When the soul has reached the end of gratification and reaped the bitter fruits of egotism, it is ready to receive the Divine Wisdom and to enter into the Divine Life. Only the crucified can be transfigured; only by the death of self can the Lord of the heart rise again into the Immortal Life, and stand radiant upon the Olivet of Wisdom.

Thou hast thy trials? Every outward trial is the replica of an inward imperfection. Thou shalt grow wise by knowing this, and shalt thereby transmute trial into active joy, finding the Kingdom where trial cannot come. When wilt thou learn thy lessons, O child of earth! All thy sorrows cry out against thee; every pain is thy just accuser, and thy griefs are but the shadows of thy unworthy and perishable self. The Kingdom of Heaven is thine; how long wilt thou reject it, preferring the lurid atmosphere of Hell — the hell of thy self-seeking self?

Where self is not there is the Garden of the Heavenly Life, and
"There spring the healing streams
Quenching all thirst! there bloom the immortal flowers
Carpeting all the way with joy! there throng Swiftest and sweetest hours!"

The redeemed sons of God, the glorified in body and spirit, are "bought with a price," and that price is the crucifixion of the personality, the death of self; and having put away that within which is the source of all discord, they have found the universal Music, the abiding Joy.

Life is more than motion, it is Music; more than rest, it is Peace; more than work, it is Duty; more than labour, it is Love; more than enjoyment, it is Blessedness; more than acquiring money and position and reputation, it is Knowledge, Purpose, strong and high Resolve.

Let the impure turn to Purity, and they shall be pure; let the weak resort to Strength, and they shall be strong; let the ignorant fly to Knowledge, and they shall be wise. All things are man's, and he chooses that which he will have. To-day he chooses in ignorance, to-morrow he shall choose in Wisdom. He shall "work out his own salvation" whether he believe it or not, for he cannot escape himself, nor transfer to another the eternal responsibility of his own soul. By no theological subterfuge shall he trick the Law of his being, which shall shatter all his selfish makeshifts and excuses for right thinking and right doing. Nor shall God do for him that which it is destined his soul shall accomplish for itself. What would you say of a man who, wanting to possess a mansion in which to dwell peacefully, purchased the site and then knelt down and asked God to build the house for him? Would you not say that such a man was foolish? And of another man who, having purchased the land, set the architects and builders and carpenters at work to erect the edifice, would you not say that he was wise? And as it is in the building of a material house, even so it is in the building of a spiritual mansion. Brick by brick, pure thought upon pure thought, good deed upon good deed, must the habitation of a blameless life rise from its sure foundation until at last it stands out in all the majesty of its faultless proportions. Not by caprice, nor gift, nor favour does a man obtain the spiritual realities, but by diligence, watchfulness, energy, and effort.

"Strong is the soul, and wise and beautiful;
The seeds of God-like power are in us still;
Gods are we, bards, saints, heroes, if we will."

The spiritual Heart of man is the Heart of the universe, and, finding that Heart, man finds the strength to accomplish all things. He finds there also the Wisdom to see things as they are. He finds there the Peace that is divine. At the centre of man's being is the Music which orders the stars — the Eternal Harmony. He who would find Blessedness, let him find himself; let him abandon every discordant desire, every inharmonious thought, every unlovely habit and deed, and he will find that Grace and Beauty and Harmony which form the indestructible essence of his own being.

Men fly from creed to creed, and find — unrest; they travel in many lands, and discover — disappointment; they build themselves beautiful mansions, and plant pleasant gardens, and reap — ennui and discomfort. Not until a man falls back upon the Truth within himself does he find rest and satisfaction; not until he builds the inward Mansion of Faultless Conduct does he find the endless and incorruptible Joy, and, having obtained that, he will infuse it into all his outward doings and possessions.

If a man would have peace, let him exercise the spirit of Peace; if he would find love, let him dwell in the spirit of Love; if he would escape suffering, let him cease to inflict it; if he would do noble things for humanity, let him cease to do ignoble things for himself. If he will but quarry the mine of his own soul, he shall find there all the materials for building whatsoever he will, and he shall find there also the central Rock on which to build in safety.

Howsoever a man works to right the world, it will never be righted until he has put himself right. This may be written upon the heart as a mathematical axiom. It is not enough to preach Purity, men must cease from lust; to exhort to love, they must abandon hatred; to extol self-sacrifice, they must yield up self; to adorn with mere words the Perfect Life, they must be perfect.

When a man can no longer carry the weight of his many sins, let him fly to the Christ, whose throne is the centre of his own heart, and he shall become light-hearted, entering the glad company of the Immortals.

When he can no longer bear the burden of his accumulated learning, let a man leave his books, his science, his philosophy, and come back to himself, and he shall find within, that which he outwardly sought and found not — his own divinity.

He ceases to argue about God who has found God within. Relying upon that calm strength which is not the strength of self, he lives God, manifesting in his daily life the Highest Goodness, which is Eternal Life.

2. The Eternal Now

NOW is thy reality in which time is contained. It is more and greater than time; it is an ever-present reality. It knows neither past nor future, and is eternally potent and substantial. Every minute, every day, every year is a dream as soon as it has passed, and exists only as an imperfect and unsubstantial picture in the memory, if it be not entirely obliterated.

Past and future are dreams; now is a reality. All things are now; all power, all possibility, all action is now. Not to act and accomplish now is not to act and accomplish at all. To live in thoughts of what you might have done, or in dreams of what you mean to do, this is folly: but to put away regret, to anchor anticipation, and to do and to work now, this is wisdom.

Whilst a man is dwelling upon the past or future he is missing the present; he is forgetting to live now. All things are possible now, and only now. Without wisdom to guide him, and mistaking the unreal for the real, a man says, "If I had done so and so last week, last month, or last year, it would have been better with me to-day"; or, "I know what is best to be done, and I will do it to-morrow." The selfish cannot comprehend the vast importance and value of the present, and fail to see it as the substantial reality of which past and future are the empty reflections. It may truly be said that past and future do not exist except as negative shadows, and to live in them — that is, in the regretful and selfish contemplation of them— is to miss the reality in life.

"The Present, the Present is all thou hast
For thy sure possessing;
Like the patriarch's angel, hold it fast,
Till it gives its blessing.
"All which is real now remaineth,
And fadeth never:
The hand which upholds it now sustaineth
The soul for ever.

"Then of what is to be, and of what is done,
Why queriest thou?
The past and the time to be are one,
And both are NOW!"

Man has all power now; but not knowing this, he says, "I will be perfect next year, or in so many years, or in so many lives." The dwellers in the Kingdom of God, who live only in the now, say, "I am perfect now," and refraining from all sin now, and ceaselessly guarding the portals of the mind, not looking to the past nor to the future, nor turning to the left or right, they remain eternally holy and blessed." Now is the accepted time; now is the day of salvation."

Say to yourself, "I will live in my Ideal now; I will manifest my Ideal now; I will be my Ideal now; and all that tempts me away
from my Ideal I will not listen to; I will listen only to the voice of my Ideal." Thus resolving, and thus doing, you shall not de-part from the Highest, and shall eternally manifest the True.

"Afoot and light-hearted, I take to the open road.
Henceforth I ask not good fortune: I myself am good fortune.
Henceforth I whimper no more, postpone no more, need nothing;
Done with indoor complaints, libraries, querulous criticisms.
Strong and content, I take to the open road."

Cease to tread every byway of dependence, every winding side-way that tempts thy soul into the shadow-land of the past and the future, and manifest thy native and divine strength now. Come out into" the open road. "That which you would be, and hope to be you may be now. Non-accomplishment resides in your perpetual postponement, and, having the power to postpone, you also have the power to accomplish — to perpetually accomplish: realize this truth, and you shall be to-day, and every day, the ideal man of whom you dreamed.

Virtue consists in fighting sin day after day. but holiness consists in leaving sin, Unnoticed and ignored, to die by the wayside; and this is done, can only be done, in the living now. Say not unto thy soul, "Thou shall be purer to-morrow"; but rather say, "Thou shalt be pure now." To-morrow is too late for anything, and he who sees his help and salvation in to-morrow shall continually fail and fall to-day.

Thou didst fall yesterday? Didst sin grievously? Having realized this, leave it. instantly-and forever, and watch that thou sinnest not now. The while thou art bewailing the past, every gate of thy soul remains unguarded against the entrance of sin now. Thou shalt not rise by grieving over the irremediable past, but by remedying the present.

The foolish man, loving the boggy side-path of procrastination rather than the firm Highway of Present Effort, says, "I will rise early to-morrow; I will get out of debt to-morrow; I will carry out my intentions to-morrow." But the wise man, realizing the momentous import of the Eternal Now, rises early to-day; keeps out of debt to-day; carries out his intentions to-day; and so never departs from strength and peace and ripe accomplishment.

That which is done now remains; that which is to be done to-morrow does not appear. It is wisdom to leave that which has not arrived, and to attend to that which is; and to attend to it with such a consecration of soul and concentration of effort as shall leave no possible loophole for regret to creep in.

A man's spiritual comprehension being clouded by the illusions of self, he says, "I was born on such a day, so many years ago, and shall die at my allotted time." But he was not born, neither will he die, for how can that which is immortal, which eternally is, be subject to birth and death? Let a man throw off his illusions, and then he will see that the birth and death of the body are the mere incidents of a journey, and not its beginning and end.

Looking back to happy beginnings, and forward to mournful endings, a man's eyes are blinded, so that he beholds not his own immortality; his ears are closed, so that he hears not the ever-present harmonies of Joy; and his heart is hardened, so that it pulsates not to the rhythmic sounds of Peace.

The universe, with all that it contains, is now. Put out thy hand, O man, and receive the fruits of Wisdom! Cease from thy greedy striving, thy selfish sorrowing, thy foolish regretting, and he content to live.

Act now, and, lo! all things are done; live now, and, behold! thou art in the midst of Plenty; be now, and know that thou art perfect.

3. The "Original Simplicity"

LIFE is simple. Being is simple. The universe is simple. Complexity arises in ignorance and self-delusion. The "Original Simplicity" of Lao-tze is a term expressive of the universe as it is, and not as it appears. Looking through the woven network of his own illusions, man sees interminable complication and unfathomable mystery, and so loses himself in the labyrinths of his own making. Let a man put away egotism, and he will see the universe in all the beauty of its pristine simplicity. Let him annihilate the delusion of the personal "I," and he will destroy all the illusions which spring from that "I." He will thus "re-become a little child," and will "revert to Original Simplicity."

When a man succeeds in entirely forgetting (annihilating) his personal self, he be-comes a mirror in which the universal Reality is faultlessly reflected. He is awakened, and henceforward he lives, not in dreams, but realities.

Pythagoras saw the universe in the ten numbers, but even this simplicity may be further reduced, and the universe ultimately be found to be contained in the number ONE, for all the numerals and all their infinite complications are but additions of the One.

Let life cease to be lived as a fragmentary thing, and let it be lived as a perfect Whole; the simplicity of the Perfect will then be revealed. How shall the fragment comprehend the Whole? Yet how simple that the Whole should comprehend the fragment. How shall sin perceive Holiness? Yet how plain that Holiness should understand sin. He who would become the Greater let him abandon the lesser. In no form is the circle contained, but in the circle all forms are contained. In no colour is the radiant light imprisoned, but in the radiant light all colours are embodied, Let a man destroy all the forms of self, and he shall apprehend the Circle of Perfection; let him submerge, in the silent depths of his being, the varying colours of his thoughts and desires, and he shall be illuminated with the White Light of Divine Knowledge. In the perfect chord of music the single note, though forgotten, is indispensably contained, and the drop of water becomes of supreme usefulness by losing itself in the ocean. Sink thyself compassionately in the heart of humanity, and thou shalt reproduce the harmonies of Heaven; lose thyself in unlimited love toward all, and thou shalt work enduring works and shalt become one with the eternal Ocean of Bliss.

Man evolves outward to the periphery of complexity, and then involves backward to the Central Simplicity. When a man discovers that it is mathematically impossible for him to know the universe before knowing himself, he then starts upon the Way which leads to the Original Simplicity. He begins to unfold from within, and as he Unfolds himself, he enfolds the universe.

Cease to speculate about God, and find the all-embracing Good within thee, then shalt thou see the emptiness and vanity of speculation, knowing thyself one with God.

He who will not give up his secret lust, his covetousness, his anger, his opinion about this or that, can see nor know nothing; he will remain a dullard in the school of Wisdom, though he be accounted learned in the colleges.

If a man would find the Key of Knowledge, let him find himself. Thy sins are not thyself; they are not any part of thyself; they are diseases which thou hast come to love. Cease to cling to them, and they will no longer cling to thee. Let them fall away, and thy self shall stand revealed. Thou shalt then know thyself as Comprehensive Vision, Invincible Principle, Immortal Life, and Eternal Good.

The impure man believes impurity to be his rightful condition, but the pure man knows himself as pure being; he also, penetrating the Veils, sees all others as pure being. Purity is extremely simple, and needs no argument to support it; impurity is interminably complex, and is ever involved in defensive argument. Truth lives itself. A blameless life is the only witness of Truth. Men cannot see, and will not accept the witness until they find it within themselves; and having found it, a man becomes silent before his fellows. Truth is so simple that it cannot be found in the region of argument and advertisement, and so silent that it is only manifested in actions.

So extremely simple is Original Simplicity, that a man must let go his hold of everything before he can perceive it. The great arch is strong by virtue of the hollowness underneath, and a wise man becomes strong and invincible by emptying himself.

Meekness, Patience, Love, Compassion, and Wisdom — these are the dominant qualities of Original Simplicity; therefore the imperfect cannot understand it. Wisdom only can apprehend Wisdom, therefore the fool says, "No man is wise." The imperfect man says, "No man can be perfect," and he therefore remains where he is. Though he live with a perfect man all his life, he shall not behold his perfection. Meekness he will call cowardice; Patience, Love, and Compassion he will see as weakness; and Wisdom will appear to him as folly. Faultless discrimination belongs to the Perfect Whole, and resides not in any part, therefore men are exhorted to refrain from judgement until they have themselves manifested the Perfect Life.

Arriving at Original Simplicity, opacity disappears, and the universal transparency becomes apparent. He who has found the indwelling Reality of his own being has found the original and universal Reality. Knowing the Divine Heart within, all hearts are known, and the thoughts of all men become his who has become the master of his own thoughts; therefore the good man does not defend himself, but moulds the minds of others to his own likeness.

As the problematical transcends crudity, so Pure Goodness transcends the problematical. All problems vanish when Pure Goodness is reached; therefore the good man is called "The slayer of illusions." What problem can vex where sin is not? O thou who strivest loudly and restest not! retire into the holy silence of thine own being, and live therefrom. So shalt thou, finding Pure Goodness, rend in twain the Veil of the Temple of Illusion, and shalt enter into the Patience, Peace, and transcendent Glory of the Perfect, for Pure Goodness and Original Simplicity are one.

4. The Unfailing Wisdom

A MAN should be superior to his possessions, his body, his circumstances and surroundings, and the opinions of others, and their attitude towards him. Until he is this, he is not strong and steadfast. He should also rise superior to his own desires and opinions; and until he is this, he is not wise.

The man who identifies himself with his possessions will feel that all is lost when these are lost; he who regards himself as the outcome and the tool of circumstances will weakly fluctuate with every change in his outward condition; and great will be his unrest and pain who seeks to stand upon the approbation of others.

To detach oneself from every outward thing, and to rest securely upon the inward Virtue, this is the Unfailing Wisdom. Having this Wisdom, a man will be the same whether in riches or poverty. The one cannot add to his strength, nor the other rob him of his serenity. Neither can riches defile him who has washed away all the inward defilement, nor the lack of them degrade him who has ceased to degrade the temple of his soul.

To refuse to be enslaved by any outward thing or happening, regarding all such things and happenings as for your use, for your education, this is Wisdom. To the wise all occurrences are good, and, having no eye for evil, they grow wiser every day. They utilize all things, and thus put all things under their feet. They see all their mistakes as soon as made, and accept them as lessons of intrinsic value, knowing that are no mistakes in the Divine Order. They thus rapidly approach the Divine Perfection. They are moved by none, yet learn from all. They crave love from none, yet give love to all. To learn, and not to be shaken; to love where one is not Loved : herein lies the strength which shall never fail a man. The man who says in his heart, "I will teach all men, and learn from none," will neither teach nor learn whilst he is in that frame of mind, but will remain in his folly.

All strength and wisdom and power and knowledge a man will find within himself, but. he will not find it in egotism; he will only find it in obedience, submission, and willingness to learn. He must obey the Higher, and not glorify himself in the lower. He who stands upon egotism, rejecting reproof, instruction, and the lessons of experience, will surely fall; yea, he is already fallen. Said a great Teacher to his disciples, "Those who shall be a lamp unto them-selves, relying upon themselves only, and not relying upon any external help, but holding fast to the Truth as their lamp, and, seeking their salvation in the Truth alone, shall not look for assistance to any besides themselves, it is they among my disciples who shall reach the very topmost height! But they must be willing to learn." The wise man is always anxious to learn, but never anxious to teach, for he knows that the true Teacher is in the heart of every man, and must ultimately be found there by all. The foolish man, being governed largely by vanity, is very anxious to teach, but un-unwilling to learn, not having found the Holy Teacher within who speaks wisdom to the humbly listening soul. Be self-reliant, but let thy self-reliance be saintly and not selfish.

Folly and wisdom, weakness and strength are within a man, and not in any external thing, neither do they spring from any external cause. A man cannot be strong for another, he can only be strong for himself; he cannot overcome for another, he can only overcome of himself. You may learn of another, but you must accomplish for yourself. Put away all external props, and rely upon thy Truth within you. A creed will not bear a man up in the hour of temptation; he must possess the inward Knowledge which slays temptation. A speculative philosophy will prove a shadowy thing in the time of calamity; a man must have the inward Wisdom which puts an end to grief.

Goodness, which is the aim of all religions, is distinct from religions themselves. Wisdom, which is the aim of every philosophy, is distinct from all philosophies. The Unfailing Wisdom is found only by constant practice in pure thinking and well-doing; by harmonizing one's mind and heart to those things which are beautiful, lovable, and true.

In whatever condition a man finds himself, he can always find the True; and he can find it only by so utilizing his present condition as to become strong and wise. The effeminate hankering after rewards, and the craven fear of punishment, let them be put away forever, and let a man joyfully bend himself to the faithful performance of all his duties, forgetting himself and his worthless pleasures, and living strong and pure and self-contained; so shall he surely find the Unfailing Wisdom, the God-like Patience and strength. "The situation that has not its Duty, its Ideal, was never yet occupied by man. . . . Here or nowhere is thy Ideal. Work it out therefrom, and, working, believe, live, be free. The Ideal is in thyself, the impediment, too, is in thyself: thy condition is but the stuff thou art to shape that same Ideal out of. What matters whether such stuff be of this sort or that, so the form thou give it be heroic, be poetic? Oh, thou that pinest in the imprisonment of the Actual, and criest bitterly to the gods for a kingdom wherein to rule and create, know this of a truth: the thing thou seekest is already within thee, here and now, couldest thou only see!"

All that is beautiful and blessed is in thyself, not in thy neighbour's wealth. Thou art poor? Thou art poor indeed if thou art not stronger than thy poverty! Thou hast suffered calamities? Well, wilt thou cure calamity by adding anxiety to it? Canst thou mend a broken vase by weeping over it. or restore a lost delight by thy lamentations? There is no evil but will vanish if thou wilt wisely meet it. The God-like soul does not. grieve over that which has been, is, or will be, hut perpetually rinds the Divine Good, and gains wisdom by every occurrence.

Fear is the shadow of selfishness, and cannot live where loving Wisdom is. Doubt, anxiety, and worry are unsubstantial shades in the underworld of self, and shall no more trouble him who will climb the serene altitudes of his soul. Grief, also, will be for ever dispelled by him who will comprehend the Law of his being. He who so comprehends shall find the Supreme Law of Life, and he shall find that it is Love, that it is imperishable Love. He shall become one with that Love, and loving all, with mind freed from all hatred and folly, he shall receive the invincible protection which Love affords. Claiming nothing, he shall suffer no loss; seeking no pleasure, he shall find no grief; and employing all his powers as instruments of service, he shall evermore live in the highest state of blessedness and bliss.

Know this: — thou makest and unmakest thyself; thou standest and fallest by what thou art. Thou art a slave if thou prefer-rest to be; thou art a master if thou wilt make thyself one. Build upon thy animal desires and intellectual opinions, and thou buildest upon the sand; build upon Virtue and Holiness, and no wind nor tide shall shake thy strong abode. So shall the Unfailing Wisdom uphold thee in every emergency, and the Everlasting Arms gather thee to thy peace.

"Lay up each year Thy harvest of well-doing, wealth that kings
Nor thieves can take away. When all the things
Thou callest thine, goods, pleasures, honours fall,
Thou in thy virtue shalt survive them all."

5. The Might Of Meekness

THE mountain bends not to the fiercest storm, but it shields the fledgling and the lamb; and though all men tread upon it, yet it protects them, and bears them up upon its deathless bosom. Even so is it with the meek man who, though shaken and disturbed by none, yet compassionately bends to shield the lowliest creature, and, though he may be despised, lifts all men up. and lovingly protects them.

As glorious as the mountain in its silent is the divine man in his silent Meekness; like its form, his loving comparison is expansive and sublime. Truly his body, like the mountain's base, is fixed in the valleys and the mists; but the summit of his being is eternally bathed in cloudless glory, and lives with the Silences.

He who has found Meekness has found divinity; he has realized the divine consciousness, and knows himself as divine. He also knows all others as divine, though they know it not themselves, being asleep and dreaming. Meekness is a divine quality, and as such is all powerful. The meek man overcomes by not resisting, and by allowing himself to be defeated he attains to the Supreme Conquest.

The man who conquers another by force is strong; the man who conquers himself by Meekness is mighty. He who conquers another by force will himself likewise be conquered; he who conquers himself by Meekness will never be overthrown, for the human cannot overcome the divine. The meek man is triumphant in defeat. Socrates lives the more by being put to death; in the crucified Jesus the risen Christ is revealed, and Stephen in receiving his stoning defies the hurting power of stones. That which is real cannot be destroyed, but only that which is unreal. When a man finds that within him which is real, which is constant, abiding, changeless, and eternal, he enters into that Reality, and becomes meek. All the powers of darkness will come against him. but they will do him no hurt, and will at last, depart from him.

The meek man is found in the time of trial; when other men fall he stands. His patience is not destroyed by the foolish passions of others, and when they come against him he does not "strive nor cry," He knows the utter powerlessness of all evil, having overcome it in himself, and lives in the changeless strength and power of divine Good.

Meekness is one aspect of the operation of that changeless Love which is at the Heart of all things, and is therefore an imperishable quality. He who lives in it is without fear, knowing the Highest, and having the lowest under his feet.

The meek man shines in darkness, and flourishes in obscurity. Meekness cannot boast, nor advertise itself, nor thrive on popularity. It is practised, and is seen or not seen; being a spiritual quality it is perceived only by the eye of the spirit. Those who are not spiritually awakened see it not, nor do they love it, being enamoured of, and blinded by, worldly shows and appearances. Nor does history take note of the meek man. Its glory is that of strife and self-aggrandizement; his is the glory of peace and gentleness. History chronicles the earthly, not the heavenly acts. Yet though he lives in obscurity he cannot be hidden (how can light be hid?) ; he continues to shine after he has withdrawn himself from the world, and is worshipped by the world which knew him not.

That the meek man should be neglected, abused, or misunderstood is reckoned by him as of no account, and therefore not to be considered, much less resisted. He knows that all such weapons are the flimsiest and most ineffectual of shadows. To them, therefore, who give him evil he gives good. He resists none, and thereby conquers all.

He who imagines he can be injured by others, and who seeks to justify and defend himself against them, does not understand Meekness, does not comprehend the essence and meaning of life. "He abused me, he beat me, he defeated me, he robbed me.— In those who harbour such thoughts hatred will never cease . . . for hatred ceases not by hatred at any time; hatred ceases by love." What sayest thou, thy neighbour has spoken thee falsely? Well, what of that? Can a falsity hurt thee? That which is false is false, and there is an end of it. It is without life, and without power to hurt any but him who seeks to hurt by it. It is nothing to thee that thy neighbour should speak falsely of thee, but it is much to thee that thou shouldst resist him, and seek to justify thyself, for, by so doing, thou givest life and vitality to thy neighbour's falseness, so that thou art injured and distressed. Take all evil out of thine own heart, then shalt thou see the folly of resisting it in another. Thou wilt be trodden on? Thou art trodden on already if thou thinkest thus. The injury that thou seest as coming from another comes only from thyself. The wrong thought, or word, or act of another has no power to hurt thee unless thou galvanize it into life by thy passionate resistance, and so receivest it into thyself. If any man slander me, that is his concern, not mine. I have to do with my own soul, not with my neighbour's. Though all the world misjudge me, it is no business of mine; but that I should possess my soul in Purity and Love, that is all my business. There shall be no end to strife until men cease to justify themselves. He who would have wars cease let him cease to defend any party — let him cease to defend himself. Not by strife can peace come, but by ceasing from strife. The glory of Caesar resides in the resistance of his enemies. They resist and fall. Give to Caesar that which Caesar demands, and Caesar's glory and power are gone. Thus, by submission does the meek man conquer the strong man : but it is not that outward show of submission which is slavery, it is that inward and spiritual submission which is freedom.

Claiming no rights, the meek man is not troubled with self-defence and self-justification; he lives in love, and therefore comes under the immediate and vital protection of the Great Love which is the Eternal Law of the universe. He neither claims nor seeks his own; thus do all things come to him, and all the universe shields and protects him.

He who says, "I have tried Meekness, and it has failed," has not tried Meekness. It cannot be tried as an experiment. It is only arrived at by unreserved self-sacrifice. Meekness does not consist merely in non-resistance in action; it consists pre-eminently in non-resistance in thought, in ceasing to hold or to have any selfish, condemnatory, or retaliatory thoughts. The meek man, therefore, cannot "take offence" or have his "feelings hurt," living above hatred, folly, and vanity. Meekness can never fail.

O thou who searchest for the Heavenly Life! strive after Meekness; increase thy patience and forbearance day by day; bid thy tongue cease from all harsh words; withdraw thy mind from selfish arguments, and refuse to brood upon thy wrongs: so living, thou shalt carefully tend and cultivate the pure and delicate flower of Meekness in thy heart,

until at last, its divine sweetness and purity and beauteous perfection shall be revealed to thee, and thou shalt become gentle, joyful, and strong. Repine not that thou art surrounded by irritable and selfish people; but rather rejoice that thou art so favoured as to have thine own imperfections revealed to thee, and that thou art so placed as to necessitate within thee a constant struggle for self-mastery and the attainment, of perfection. The more there is of harshness and selfishness around thee the greater is the need of thy Meekness and love. If others seek to wrong thee, all the more is it needful that thou shouldst cease from all wrong, and live in love; if others preach Meekness, humility, and love, and do not practice these, trouble not. nor be annoyed; but do thou, in the silence of thy heart, and in thy contact with others, practice these things, and they shall preach themselves. And though thou utter no declamatory word, and stand before no gathered audience, thou shalt teach the whole world. As thou becomest meek, thou shalt learn the deepest secrets of the universe. Nothing is hidden from him who overcomes himself. Into the cause of causes shalt thou penetrate, and lifting, one after another, every veil of illusion, shalt reach at last the inmost Heart of Being. Thus becoming one with Life, thou shalt know till life, and, seeing into causes, and knowing realities, thou shalt be no more anxious about thyself, and others, and the world, but shalt see that all things that are, are engines of the Great Law. Canopied with gentleness, thou shalt bless where others curse; love where others hate; forgive where others condemn; yield where others strive; give up where others grasp: lose where others gain, And in their strength they shall be weak ; and in thy weakness thou shalt be strong; yea, thou shalt mightily prevail. He that hath not unbroken gentleness hath not Truth:

"Therefore when Heaven would save a man, it enfolds him with gentleness."

6. The Righteous Man

THE righteous man is invincible. No enemy can possibly overcome or confound him; and he needs no other protection than that of his own integrity and holiness.

As it is impossible for evil to overcome Good, so the righteous man can never be brought low by the unrighteous. Slander, envy, hatred, malice can never reach him, nor cause him any suffering, and those who try to injure him only succeed ultimately in bringing ignominy upon themselves.

The righteous man, having nothing to hide, committing no acts which require stealth, and harbouring no thoughts and desires which he would not like others to know, is fearless and unashamed. His step is firm, his body upright, and his speech direct and without ambiguity. He looks everybody in the face. How can he fear any who wrongs none? How can he be ashamed before any who deceives none? And ceasing from all wrong he can never be wronged; ceasing from all deceit he can never be deceived.

The righteous man, performing all his duties with scrupulous diligence, and living above sin, is invulnerable at every point. He who has slain the inward enemies of virtue can never be brought low by any outward enemy; neither does he need to seek any protection against them, righteousness being an all-sufficient protection.

The unrighteous man is vulnerable at almost every point; living in his passions, the slave of prejudices, impulses, and ill-formed opinions, he is continually suffering (as he imagines) at the hands of others. The slanders, attacks, and accusations of others cause him great suffering because they have a basis of truth in himself; and not having the protection of righteousness, he endeavours to justify and protect himself by resorting to retaliation and specious argument, and even to subterfuge and deceit.

The partially righteous man is vulnerable at all those points where he falls short of righteousness, and should the righteous man fall from his righteousness, and give way to one sin, his invincibility is gone, for he has thereby placed himself where attack and accusation can justly reach and injure him, because he has first injured himself.

If a man suffers or is injured through the instrumentality of others, let him look to himself, and, putting aside self-pity and self-defence, he will find in his own heart the source of all his woe.

No evil can happen to the righteous man who has cut off the source of evil in himself; living in the All-Good, and abstaining from

sin in thought, word and deed, whatever happens to him is good; neither can any person, event, or circumstance cause him suffering, for the tyranny of circumstance is utterly destroyed for him who has broken the bonds of sin.

The suffering, the sorrowing, the weary, and broken-hearted ever seek a sorrowless refuge, a haven of perpetual peace. Let such fly to the refuge of the righteous life; let them come now and enter the haven of the sinless state, for sorrow cannot overtake the righteous; suffering cannot reach him who does not waste in self-seeking his spiritual substance; and he cannot be afflicted by weariness and unrest whose heart is at peace with all.

7. Perfect Love

THE Children of Light, who abide in the Kingdom of Heaven, see the universe, and all that it contains, as the manifestation of one Law — the Law of Love. They see Love as the moulding, sustaining, protecting, and perfecting Power immanent in all things animate and inanimate. To them Love is not merely and only a rule of life, it is the Law of Life, it is Life itself. Knowing this, they order their whole life in accordance with Love, not regarding their own personality. By thus practising obedience to the Highest, to divine Love, they become conscious partakers of the power of Love, and so arrive at perfect Freedom as Masters of Destiny.

The universe is preserved because Love is at the Heart of it. Love is the only preservative power. Whilst there is hatred in the heart of man, he imagines the Law to be cruel, but when his heart is mellowed by Compassion and Love, he perceives that the Law is Infinite Kindness. So kind is the Law that it protects man against his own ignorance, Man, in his puny efforts to subvert the Law by attaching undue importance to his own little personality, brings upon himself such trains of suffering that he is at last compelled, in the depth of his afflictions, to seek for Wisdom; and finding Wisdom, he finds Love, and knows it as the Law of his being, the Law of the universe. Love does not punish; man punishes himself by his own hatred; by striving to preserve evil which has no life by which to preserve itself, and by trying to subvert Love, which can neither be overcome nor destroyed, being of the substance of Life. When a man burns himself, does he accuse the fire? Therefore, when a man suffers, let him look for some ignorance or disobedience within himself.

Love is Perfect Harmony, pure Bliss, and contains, therefore, no element of suffering. Let a man think no thought and do no act which is not in accordance with pure Love, and suffering shall no more trouble him. If a man would know Love, and partake of its undying bliss, he must practice it in his heart; he must become Love.

He who always acts from the spirit of Love is never deserted, is never left in a dilemma or difficulty, for Love (impersonal Love) is both Knowledge and Power. He who has learned how to Love has learned how to master every difficulty, how to transmute every failure into success, how to clothe every event and condition in garments of blessedness and beauty.

The way to Love is by self-mastery, and, travelling that way, a man builds himself up in Knowledge as he proceeds. Arriving at Love, he enters into full possession of body and mind, by right of the divine Power which he has earned.

"Perfect Love casteth out fear." To know Love is to know that there is no harmful power in the whole Universe. Even sin itself, which the worldly and unbelieving imagine is so unconquerable, is known as a very weak and perishable thing, that shrinks away and disappears before the compelling power of Good. Perfect Love is perfect Harmlessness. And he who has destroyed, in himself, all thoughts of harm, and all desire to harm, receives the universal protection, and knows himself to be invincible.

Perfect Love is perfect Patience. Anger and irritability cannot dwell with it nor come near it. It sweetens every bitter occasion with the perfume of holiness, and transmutes trial into divine strength. Complaint, is foreign to it. He who loves bewails nothing, but accepts all things and conditions as heavenly guests; he is therefore constantly blessed, and sorrow does not overtake him.

Perfect Love is perfect Trust. He who has destroyed the desire to grasp can never be troubled with the fear of loss. Loss and gain are alike foreign to him. Steadfastly maintaining a loving attitude of mind toward all, and pursuing, in the performance of his duties, a constant and loving activity, Love protects him and evermore supplies him in fullest measure with all that he needs.

Perfect Love is perfect Power. The wisely loving heart commands without exercising any authority. All things and all men obey him who obeys the Highest. He thinks, and lo! he has already accomplished! He speaks, and behold! a world hangs upon his simple utterances! He has harmonized his thoughts with the Imperishable and Unconquerable Forces, and for him weakness and uncertainty are no more. His every thought is a purpose; his every act an accomplishment; he moves with the Great Law, not setting his puny personal will against it, and he thus becomes a channel through which the Divine Power can flow in unimpeded and beneficent expression. He has thus become Power itself.

Perfect Love is perfect Wisdom. The man who loves all is the man who knows all. Having thoroughly learned the lessons of his own heart, he knows the tasks and trials of other hearts, and adapts himself to them gently and without ostentation. Love illuminates the intellect; without it the intellect is blind and cold and lifeless. Love succeeds where the intellect fails; sees where the intellect is blind ; knows where the intellect is ignorant, Reason is only completed in Love, and is ultimately absorbed in it. Love is the Supreme Reality in the universe, and as such it contains all Truth. Infinite Tenderness enfolds and cherishes the universe; therefore is the wise man gentle and childlike and tender-hearted. He sees that the one thing which all creatures need is Love, and he gives unstintingly. He knows that all occasions require the adjusting power of Love, and he ceases from harshness.

To the eye of Love all things are revealed, not as an infinity of complex effects, but in the light of Eternal Principles, out of which spring all causes and effects, and back into which they return. "God is Love;" therefore than Love there is nothing more perfect. He who would find pure Knowledge let him find pure Love.

Perfect Love is perfect Peace. He who dwells with it has completed his pilgrimage in the underworld of sorrow. With mind calm and heart at rest, he has banished the shadows of grief, and knows the deathless Life.

If thou wouldst perfect thyself in Knowledge, perfect thyself in Love. If thou wouldst reach the Highest, ceaselessly cultivate a loving and compassionate heart.

8. Perfect Freedom

THERE is no bondage in the Heavenly Life. There is Perfect Freedom. This is its great glory. This Supreme Freedom is gained only by obedience. He who obeys the Highest cooperates with the Highest, and so masters every force within himself and every condition without. A man may choose the lower and neglect the Higher, but the Higher is never overcome by the lower: herein lies the revelation of Freedom. Let a man choose the Higher and abandon the lower; he shall then establish himself as an Overcomer, and shall realize Perfect Freedom.

To give the reins to inclination is the only slavery; to conquer oneself is the only freedom. The slave to self loves his chains, and will not have one of them broken for fear he would be depriving himself of some cherished delight. He clings to his gratifications and vanities, regarding freedom from them as an empty and undesirable condition. He thus defeats and enslaves himself.

By self-enlightenment is Perfect Freedom found. Whilst a man remains ignorant of himself, of his desires, of his emotions and thoughts, and of the inward causes which mould his life and destiny, having neither control nor understanding of himself, he will remain in bondage to passion, sorrow, suffering, and fluctuating fortune. The Land of Perfect Freedom lies through the Gate of Knowledge.

All outward oppression is but the shadow and effect of the real oppression within. For ages the oppressed have cried for liberty, and a thousand man-made statutes have failed to give it to them. They can give it only to themselves; they shall find it only in obedience to the Divine Statutes which are inscribed upon their hearts. Let them resort to the inward Freedom, and the shadow of oppression shall no more darken the earth. Let men cease to oppress themselves, and no man shall oppress his brother.

Men legislate for an outward freedom, yet continue to render such freedom impossible of achievement by fostering an inward condition of enslavement. They thus pursue a shadow without, and ignore the substance within. Man will be free when he is freed from self. All outward forms of bondage and oppression will cease to be when man ceases to be the willing bond-slave of passion, error, and ignorance. Freedom is to the free.

Whilst men cling to weakness they cannot have strength; whilst they love darkness they can receive no light; and so long as they prefer bondage they can enjoy no liberty. Strength, light, and freedom are ready now, and can be had by all who love them, who aspire to them. Freedom does not reside in cooperative aggression, for this will always produce, reactively, cooperative defence — warfare, hatred, party strife, and the destruction of liberty. Freedom resides in individual self-conquest. The emancipation of Humanity is frustrated and withheld by the self-enslavement of the unit. Thou who criest to man and God for liberty, liberate thyself!

The Heavenly Freedom is freedom from passion, from cravings, from opinions, from the tyranny of the flesh, and the tyranny of the intellect — this first, and then all outward freedom, as effect to cause. The Freedom that begins within, and extends outwardly until it embraces the whole man, is an emancipation so complete, all-embracing, and perfect as to leave no galling fetter unbroken. Free thy soul from all sin, and thou shalt walk a freed and fearless man in the midst of a world of fearful slaves; and, seeing thee, many slaves shall take heart and shall join thee in thy glorious freedom.

He who says, "My worldly duties are irksome to me: I will leave them and go into solitude, where I shall be as free as the air," and thinks to gain freedom thus, will find only a harder slavery. The tree of Freedom is rooted in Duty, and he who would pluck its sweet fruits must discover joy in Duty.

Glad-hearted, calm, and ready for all tasks is he who is freed from self. Irksomeness and weariness cannot enter his heart, and his divine strength lightens every burden so that its weight is not felt. He does not run away from Duty with his chains about him, but breaks them and stands free.

Make thyself pure; make thyself proof against weakness, temptation, and sin; for only in thine own heart and mind shalt thou find that Perfect Freedom for which the whole world sighs and seeks in vain.

9. Greatness And Goodness

GOODNESS, simplicity, greatness — these three are one, and this trinity of perfection cannot be separated. All greatness springs from goodness, and all goodness is profoundly simple, Without goodness there is no greatness. Some men pass through the world as destructive forces, like the tornado or the avalanche, but they are not great; they are to greatness as the avalanche is to the mountain. The work of greatness is enduring and preservative, and not violent and destructive. The greatest souls are the most gentle.

Greatness is never obtrusive. It works in silence, seeking no recognition. This is why it is not easily perceived and recognized. Like the mountain, it towers up in its vastness, so that those in its immediate vicinity, who receive its shelter and shade, do not see it. Its sublime grandeur is only beheld as they recede from it. The great man is not seen by his contemporaries; the majesty of his form is only outlined by its recession in time. This is the awe and enchantment of distance. Men occupy themselves with the small things; their houses, trees, lands. Few contemplate the mountain at whose base they live, and fewer still essay to explore it. But in the distance these small thing disappear, and then the solitary beauty of the mountain is perceived. Popularity, noisy obtrusiveness, and shallow show, these superficialities rapidly disappear, and leave behind no enduring mark: whereas greatness slowly emerges from obscurity, and endures for ever.

Jewish Rabbi and rabble alike saw not the divine beauty of Jesus; they saw only an unlettered carpenter. To his acquaintances, Homer was only a blind beggar, but the centuries reveal him as Homer the immortal poet. Two hundred years after the farmer of Stratford (and all that is known of him) has disappeared, the real Shakespeare is discerned. All true genius is impersonal. It belongs not to the man through whom it is manifested; it belongs to all. It is a diffusion of pure Truth: the Light of Heaven descending on all mankind.

Every work of genius, in whatsoever department of art, is a symbolic manifestation of impersonal Truth. It is universal, and finds a response in every heart in every age and race. Anything short of this is not genius, is not greatness. That work which defends a religion perishes; it is religion that lives. Theories about immortality fade away; immortal man endures; commentaries upon Truth come to the dust; Truth alone remains. That only is true in art which represents the True; that only is great in life which is universally and eternally true. And the True is the Good; the Good is the True.

Every immortal work springs from the Eternal Goodness in the human heart, and it is clothed with the sweet and unaffected simplicity of goodness. The greatest art is, like nature, artless. It knows no trick, no pose, no studied effort. There are no stage-tricks in Shakespeare; and he is the greatest of dramatists because he is the simplest. The critics, not understanding the wise simplicity of greatness, always condemn the loftiest work. They cannot discriminate between the childish and the childlike. The True, the Beautiful, the Great, is always childlike, and is perennially fresh and young.

The great man is always the good man; he is always simple. He draws from, nay, lives in, the inexhaustible fountain of divine Goodness within; he inhabits the Heavenly Places; communes with the vanished great ones; lives with the Invisible: he is inspired, and breathes the airs of Heaven.

He who would be great let him learn to be good. He will therefore become great by not seeking greatness. Aiming at greatness a man arrives at nothingness; aiming at nothingness he arrives at greatness. The desire to be great is an indication of littleness, of personal vanity and obtrusiveness. The willingness to disappear from gaze, the utter absence of self-aggrandizement is the witness of greatness.

Littleness seeks and loves authority. Greatness is never authoritative, and it thereby becomes the authority to which the after ages appeal. He who seeks, loses; he who is willing to lose, wins all men. Be thy simple self, thy better self, thy impersonal self, and lo! thou art great! He who selfishly seeks authority shall succeed only in becoming a trembling apologist courting protection behind the back of acknowledged greatness. He who will become the servant of all men, desiring no personal authority, shall live as a man, and shall be called great. "Abide in the simple and noble regions of thy life, obey thy heart, and thou shalt reproduce the foreworld again." Forget thine own little self, and fall back upon the Universal self, and thou shalt reproduce, in living and enduring forms, a thousand beautiful experiences; thou shalt find within thyself that simple goodness which is greatness.

"It is as easy to be great as to be small," says Emerson; and he utters a profound truth. Forgetfulness of self is the whole of greatness, as it is the whole of goodness and happiness. In a fleeting moment of self-forgetfulness the smallest soul becomes great; extend that moment indefinitely, and there is a great soul, a great life. Cast away thy personality (thy petty cravings, vanities, and ambitions) as a worthless garment, and dwell in the loving, compassionate, selfless regions of thy soul, and thou art no longer small—thou art great.

Claiming personal authority, a man descends into littleness; practising goodness, a man ascends into greatness. The presumptuousness of the small may, for a time, obscure the humility of the great, but it is at last swallowed up by it, as the noisy river is lost in the calm ocean.

The vulgarity of ignorance and the pride of learning must disappear. Their worthlessness is equal. They have no part in the Soul of Goodness. If thou wouldst do, thou must be. Thou shalt not mistake information for Knowledge; thou must know thyself as pure Knowledge. Thou shalt not confuse learning with Wisdom; thou must apprehend thyself as undefiled Wisdom.

Wouldst thou write a living book? Thou must first live; thou shalt draw around thee the mystic garment of a manifold experience, and shalt learn, in enjoyment and suffering, gladness and sorrow, conquest and defeat, that which no book and no teacher can teach thee. Thou shalt learn of life, of thy soul; thou shalt tread the Lonely Road, and shalt become; thou shalt be. Thou shalt then write thy book, and it shall live; it shall be more than a book. Let thy book first live in thee, then shalt thou live in thy book.

Wouldst thou carve a statue that shall captivate the ages, or paint a picture that shall endure? Thou shalt acquaint thyself with the divine Beauty within thee. Thou shalt comprehend and adore the Invisible Beauty ; thou shalt know the Principles which are the soul of Form; thou shalt perceive the matchless symmetry and faultless proportions of Life, of Being, of the Universe; thus knowing the eternally True thou shalt carve or paint the indescribably Beautiful.

Wouldst thou produce an imperishable poem? Thou shalt first live thy poem; thou shalt think and act rhythmically; thou shalt find the never-failing source of inspiration in the loving places of thy heart. Then shall immortal lines flow from thee without effort, and. as the flowers of wood and field spontaneously spring, so shall beautiful thoughts grow up in thine heart and, enshrined in words as moulds to their beauty, shall subdue the hearts of men.

Wouldst thou compose such music as shall gladden and uplift the world? Thou shalt adjust thy soul to the Heavenly Harmonies. Thou shalt know that thyself, that life and the universe is Music. Thou shalt touch the chords of Life. Thou shalt know that Music is everywhere; that it is the Heart of Being; then shalt thou hear with thy spiritual ear the Deathless Symphonies.

Wouldst thou preach the living word? Thou shalt forego thyself, and become that Word. Thou shalt know one thing—that the human heart is good, is divine; thou shalt live on one thing—Love. Thou shalt love all, seeing no evil, thinking no evil, believing no evil; then, though thou speak but little, thy every act shall be a power, thy every word a precept. By thy pure thought, thy selfless deed, though it appear hidden, thou shalt preach, down the ages, to untold multitudes of aspiring souls.

To him who chooses Goodness, sacrificing all, is given that which is more than and includes all. He becomes the possessor of the Best, communes with the Highest, and enters the company of the Great.

The greatness that is flawless, rounded, and complete is above and beyond all art. It is Perfect Goodness in manifestation; therefore the greatest souls are always Teachers.

10. Heaven In The Heart

THE toil of life ceases when the heart is pure. When the mind is harmonized with the Divine Law the wheel of drudgery ceases to turn, and all work is transmuted into joyful activity. The pure-hearted are as the lilies of the field, which toil not, yet are fed and clothed from the abundant storehouse of the All-Good. But the lily is not lethargic; it is ceaselessly active, drawing nourishment from earth and air and sun. By the Divine Power immanent within it, it builds itself up, cell by cell, opening itself to the light, growing and expanding towards the perfect flower. So is it with those who, having yielded up self-will, have learned to cooperate with the Divine Will. They grow in grace, goodness, and beauty, freed from anxiety, and without friction and toil. And they never work in vain; there is no waste action. Every thought, act, and thing done subserves the Divine Purpose, and adds to the sum-total of the world's happiness.

Heaven is in the heart. They will look for it in vain who look elsewhere. In no outward place will the soul find Heaven until it finds it within itself; for, wherever the soul goes, its thoughts and desires will go with it; and, howsoever beautiful may be its outward dwelling-place, if there is sin within, there will be darkness and gloom without, for sin always casts a dark shadow over the pathway of the soul—the shadow of sorrow.

This world is beautiful, transcendently and wonderfully beautiful. Its beauties and inspiring wonders cannot be numbered; yet, to the sin-sodden mind, it appears as a dark and joyless place. Where passion and self are, there is hell, and there are all the pains of hell; where Holiness and Love are, there is Heaven, and there are all the joys of Heaven.

Heaven is here. It is also everywhere. It is wherever there is a pure heart. The whole universe is abounding with joy, but the sin-bound heart can neither see, hear, nor partake of it. No one is, or can be, arbitrarily shut out from Heaven; each shuts himself out. Its Golden Gates are eternally ajar, but the selfish cannot find them; they mourn, yet see not; they cry, but hear not. Only to those who turn their eyes to heavenly things, their ears to heavenly sounds, are the happy Portals of the Kingdom revealed, and they enter and are glad.

All life is gladness when the heart is right, when it is attuned to the sweet chords of holy Love. Life is Religion, Religion is life and all is Joy and Gladness. The jarring notes of creeds and parties, the black shadows of sin, let them pass away for ever; they cannot enter the Door of Life; they form no part of Religion. Joy, Music, Beauty—these belong to the True Order of things; they are of the texture of the universe; of these is the divine Garment of Life woven. Pure Religion is glad, not gloomy. It is Light without darkness or shadow.

Despondency, disappointment, grief — these are the reflex aspects of pleasurable excitement, self-seeking, and desire. Give up the latter, and the former will for ever disappear; then there remains the perfect Bliss of Heaven.

Abounding and unalloyed Happiness is man's true life; perfect Blessedness is his rightful portion ; and when he loses his false life and finds the true he enters into the full possession of his Kingdom. The Kingdom of Heaven is man's Home; and it is here and now, it is in his own heart, and he is not left without Guides, if he wills to find it. All man's sorrows and sufferings are the result of his own self-elected estrangement from the Divine Source, the All-Good, the Father, the

Heart of Love. Let him return to his Home; his peace awaits him.

The Heavenly-hearted are without sorrow and suffering, because they are without sin. What the worldly-minded call troubles they regard as pleasant tasks of Love and Wisdom. Troubles belong to hell; they do not enter Heaven. This is so simple it should not appear strange. If you have a trouble it is in your own mind, and nowhere else; you make it, it is not made for you; it is not in your task; it is not in that outward thing. You are its creator, and it derives its life from you only. Look upon all your difficulties as lessons to be learned, as aids to spiritual growth, and lo! they are difficulties no longer! This is one of the Pathways up to Heaven.

To transmute everything into Happiness and Joy, this is supremely the work and duty of the Heavenly-minded man. To reduce everything to wretchedness and deprivation is the process which the worldly-minded unconsciously pursue. To live in Love is to work in Joy. Love is the magic that transforms all things into power and beauty. It brings plenty out of poverty, power out of weakness, loveliness out of deformity, sweetness out of bitterness, light out of darkness, and produces all blissful conditions out of its own substantial but indefinable essence.

He who loves can never want. The universe belongs to Goodness, and it therefore belongs to the good man. It can be possessed by all without stint or shrinking, for Goodness, and the abundance of Goodness (material, mental, and spiritual abundance), is inexhaustible. Think lovingly, speak lovingly, act lovingly, and your every need shall be supplied; you shall not walk in desert places, and no danger shall overtake you.

Love sees with faultless vision, judges true judgement, acts in wisdom. Look through the eyes of Love, and you shall see everywhere the Beautiful and True; judge with the mind of Love, and you shall err not, shall wake no wail of sorrow; act in the spirit of Love, and you shall strike undying harmonies upon the Harp of Life.

Make no compromise with self. Cease not to strive until your whole being is swallowed up in Love. To love all and always—this is the Heaven of heavens. "Let there be nothing within thee that is not very beautiful and very gentle, and then will there be nothing without thee that is not beautified and softened by the spell of thy presence." All that you do, let it be done in calm wisdom, and not from desire, impulse, or opinion; this is the Heavenly way of action.

Purify your thought-world until no stain is left, and you will ascend into Heaven while living in the body. You will then see the things of the outward world clothed in all beautiful forms. Having found the Divine Beauty within ourselves, it springs to life in every outward thing. To the beautified soul the world is beautiful.

Undeveloped souls are merely unopened flowers. The perfect Beauty lies concealed within, and will one day reveal itself to the full-orbed light of Heaven. Seeing men thus, we stand where evil is not, and where the eye beholds only good. Herein lies the peace and patience and beauty of Love—it sees no evil. He who loves thus becomes the protector of all men. Though in their ignorance they should hate him, he shields and loves them.

What gardener is so foolish as to condemn his flowers because they do not develop in a day? Learn to love, and you shall see in all souls, even those called "degraded," the Divine Beauty, and shall know that it will not fail to come forth in its own season. This is one of the Heavenly Visions; it is out of this that Gladness comes.

Sin, sorrow, suffering — these are the dark gropings of the unopened soul for Light. Open the petals of your soul and let the glorious Light stream in.

Every sinful soul is an unresolved harmony. It shall at last strike the Perfect Chord, and swell the joyful melodies of Heaven.

Hell is the preparation for Heaven; and out of the debris of its ruined hovels are built pleasant mansions wherein the perfected soul may dwell.

Night is only a fleeting shadow which the world casts, and sorrow is but a transient shade cast by the self. "Come out into the Sunlight." Know this, O reader! that you are divine. You are not cut off from the Divine except in your own unbelief. Rise up, O Son of God! and shake off the nightmare of sin which binds you; accept your heritage—the Kingdom of Heaven! Drug your soul no longer with the poisons of false beliefs. You are not "a worm of the dust" unless you choose to make yourself one. You are a divine, immortal, God-born being, and this you may know if you will to seek and find. Cling no longer to your impure and grovelling thoughts, and you shall know that you are a radiant and celestial spirit, filled with all pure and lovable thoughts. Wretchedness and sin and sorrow are not your portion here unless you accept them as such; and if you do this, they will be your portion hereafter, for these things are not apart from your soul-condition: they will go wherever you go; they are only within you.

Heaven, not hell, is your portion here and always. It only requires you to take that which belongs to you. You are the master, and you choose whom you will serve. You are the maker of your state, and your choice determines your condition. What you pray and ask for (with your mind and heart, not with your lips merely), this you receive. You are served as you serve. You are conditioned as you condition. You garner in your own.

Heaven is yours; you have but to enter in and take possession; and Heaven means Supreme Happiness, Perfect Blessedness; it leaves nothing to be desired; nothing to be grieved over. It is complete satisfaction now and in this world. It is within you ; and if you do not know this, it is because you persist in turning the back of your soul upon it. Turn round and you shall behold it.

Come and live in the sunshine of your being. Come out of the shadows and the dark places. You are framed for Happiness. You are a child of Heaven. Purity, Wisdom, Love, Plenty, Joy, and Peace—these are the eternal Realities of the Kingdom, and they are yours, but you cannot possess them in sin; they have no part in the Realm of Darkness. They belong to "the Light which lighteth every man that cometh into the world," the Light of spotless Love. They are the heritage of the holy Christ-Child who shall come to birth in your soul when you are ready to divest yourself of all your impurities. They are your real self.

But he whose soul has been safely delivered of the Wonderful Joy-Child does not forget the travail of the world.

Printed in Great Britain
by Amazon